BUILDING A STANDARD
SUNDAY SCHOOL

BUILDING
A STANDARD
SUNDAY SCHOOL

Arthur Flake

CONVENTION PRESS

Nashville, Tennessee

Printed in the United States of America
15. N 55 R.R.D.

PREFACE

THE Standard of Excellence erected by the Baptist Sunday School Board, by which Sunday schools may test their efficiency, is more and more demonstrating its value. The effects of its influence are seen, not only in the high quality of the work done by schools which measure up to the Standard requirements, but also in the rapid improvement in the work of Sunday schools upon adopting the Standard of Excellence as a working basis.

Indeed so valuable as a working basis for a Sunday school does the adoption of the Standard of Excellence seem that it has been considered advisable to devote this study to a consideration of the subject in all its varied phases. Therefore, the purpose in producing this book is threefold, viz.: To help to a better understanding of the meaning of each point in the Standard of Excellence, to give in the minutest detail instructions concerning how to meet each one of the requirements, and to present at the same time a full discussion of plans and methods for building a great Sunday school.

This study deals with the Sunday school situation mainly from the standpoint of the officers. However, it is essential that the teachers should also understand thoroughly the principles and methods of Sunday school administration in order that they may intelligently co-operate with the officers in their plans to build the Sunday school. Therefore, it is suggested that Sunday school teachers also should make a study of this book.

A. F.

CONTENTS

THE SUNDAY SCHOOL TRAINING COURSE

The Sunday School Training Course prepared by the Sunday School Department of the Baptist Sunday School Board is one of the major means of promoting Sunday school work. Its influence is limited only by its use.

The six sections of the course include studies in Bible, doctrines, evangelism, Sunday school leadership and administration, teaching, age group studies, and special studies. The range of the course is broad, for the field of Sunday school work is broad and requires comprehensive and specific training. Sixteen books are required for the completion of each diploma.

The study of the training course is not to be limited to the present Sunday school workers. Most churches need twice as many workers as are now enlisted. This need can be supplied by training additional workers now. Members of the Young People's and Adult classes and older Intermediates should be led to study these books, for thereby will their service be assured. Parents will find help as they study what the Sunday school is trying to do.

SPECIAL NOTE TO INSTRUCTORS:

During your teaching of this book will you check with the Sunday school superintendent and see if an accurate record of training for the workers is kept. If not, please urge him to set up such a file with an associate superintendent of training in charge. File cards for this purpose may be purchased at a nominal cost from your nearest Baptist Book Store.

> A. V. WASHBURN
> *Secretary, Teaching and Training,*
> *Sunday School Department, Baptist*
> *Sunday School Board*

1

THE STANDARD OF EXCELLENCE: ITS DESIGN, AIM, AND VALUE

THE THEME of this study is the program of work for Southern Baptist Sunday schools as it is set out in the first Standard of Excellence as offered by the Sunday School Board of the Southern Baptist Convention. The idea of having a Standard includes both the measuring of work and the recognition of achievement. It is nowhere intended that the attainment of this Standard shall be considered as an end within itself, but it is intended as a means to an end—namely, the building of bigger and better Sunday schools. In this chapter we are to consider the design, aim, and value of this Standard of Excellence.

I. THE DESIGN OF THE STANDARD OF EXCELLENCE

The Sunday School Board has erected two Standards by which Sunday schools measure their efficiency—the first Standard and the Advanced Standard.

The first Standard deals with the great Sunday school fundamentals and is designed with a view of providing a practical program of work easily adaptable for use in every Sunday school within the confines of the territory of the Convention. It will meet the needs of the hundreds and thousands of Sunday schools with limited possibilities, both numerically and financially, and will encourage them to strive to attain unto the best. It incorporates in its ten requirements the fundamental qualities of an efficient Sunday school. However, it requires neither a complex department and class organization nor elaborate and expensive equipment.

Sunday schools which are blessed with good equipment and large department organizations should not regard lightly the first Standard because it does not emphasize these two points. They should see that they are meeting faithfully the requirements in the first Standard, then set the Advanced Standard before them and go on to its attainment.

STANDARD OF EXCELLENCE FOR BAPTIST SUNDAY SCHOOLS

STANDARD RECOGNITION

will be granted for the Sunday school year in which the application is dated:

1. When the school maintains Standard efficiency for at least one month and the leaders of the Sunday school are satisfied that Standard work is being done.

2. When the school agrees to follow these principles for the remainder of the Sunday school year. An additional Standard efficiency award will be granted at the close of the Sunday school year provided the school maintains Standard efficiency for any nine months in the Sunday school year and requests the award.

3. When the application is made upon the form provided, endorsed by the state Sunday school secretary, and approved by the Sunday School Department of the Baptist Sunday School Board.

I. Church Relationship

1. The church shall elect the officers and teachers.

2. The school shall make monthly or quarterly reports to the church.

II. Enlargement

1. The enrolment of the school shall at least equal the number of resident church members as recognized by the church.

2. The school shall promote a program of visitation.

III. Grading

The school shall be graded as follows: Cradle Roll, birth through 3; Beginners, 4-5; Primaries, 6-8; Juniors, 9-12; Intermediates, 13-16; Young People, 17-24; Adults, 25 and above; and an Extension department for those who cannot attend.

(Note.—If possible one or more Nurseries should be provided for children, birth through three.)

IV. Baptist Literature

Southern Baptist Sunday school literature prepared for the teachers and pupils in the various age groups shall be used throughout the school.

V. Bibles

1. The Bible shall be used as the textbook of the school.
2. The officers and teachers shall provide opportunities for the pupils to use their Bibles in the school.
3. The officers and teachers shall encourage the pupils and their parents to engage in daily family Bible reading and prayer.

VI. Preaching Attendance

1. An average of at least 70 per cent of the officers, teachers, and pupils above eight years of age attending the school shall remain for the preaching services.
2. The Beginners and Primaries shall be encouraged to remain for the preaching services.

VII. Evangelism

1. The school shall be positively evangelistic.
2. The teachers shall earnestly seek to lead their pupils who are not Christians to a personal acceptance of Christ as Saviour and Lord.
3. The superintendent and pastor shall give frequent opportunities for the pupils who are not Christians to confess Christ publicly, and urge them to do so.

VIII. Meetings, Equipment, and Records

1. The school shall maintain a weekly officers and teachers' meeting or a monthly workers' conference.
2. The Sunday sessions of the school shall be at least one hour in length, preferably one hour and fifteen minutes.
3. Each age group below the Intermediates shall be separated from the remainder of the school at least for the class sessions by walls, movable partitions, screens, or curtains.
4. At least 50 per cent of the classes above the Juniors shall be separated from the remainder of the school for the class sessions by walls, movable partitions, screens, or curtains.
5. The school shall use the Six Point Record System.

IX. Training

1. The school shall conduct at least one training school each year, completing at least one book in the Sunday School Training Course.
2. At least 50 per cent of the officers and teachers, including the pastor or superintendent, shall hold an award for either *Building a Standard Sunday School* or *A Church Using Its Sunday School*.

3. At least 50 per cent of the officers and teachers, including the pastor or superintendent, shall hold an award for at least one other book in the Sunday School Training Course.

X. Stewardship and Missions

1. The school shall support the church program and promote the general missionary, educational, and benevolent causes fostered by the denomination.

2. The school shall present educationally each year at least four denominational causes, and shall provide opportunities for the members to contribute to each of these causes in accordance with the policy of the church.

A good Sunday school is not an accident. It must be built. In order to build a good Sunday school three things are necessary.

First, the essentials of a good Sunday school must be known.

Second, the plans for building a good Sunday school must be understood.

Third, the specifications for building a good Sunday school must be faithfully followed.

II. The Twofold Aim of the Standard of Excellence

1. *To Set Out the Essentials of a Good Sunday School*

The leaders should be informed as to the things which go to make up an efficient Sunday school. The qualities which make for efficiency should be kept before the school to guide the officers and teachers in building the school.

The Standard of Excellence presents these. It emphasizes certain fundamental things which should characterize a good Sunday school, such as the school's relation to the church, its enrolment, its literature, its Bible study, its work in winning souls, its denominational affiliation, and other worth-while things.

2. *To Present Plans for Building a Good Sunday School*

Knowing the essentials of a good Sunday school is not enough; the plans for building such a school must be understood. Vagueness, indefiniteness, and aimlessness always hinder progress. A good Sunday school can no more be built without the builder having well-defined plans to work by than a watch that will keep correct time can be made by throwing the material together without a plan and a working knowledge of that plan.

The plans suggested by the Standard of Excellence for building an efficient Sunday school are simple and workable and will greatly aid if they are properly understood and utilized.

Note again some of the things which must be used in planning to build a Standard Sunday school. The school must be under church control; it must be graded; the building must be arranged for teaching; the best literature must be used; Bibles must be used; the officers and teachers must be trained; a weekly officers and teachers' meeting or a monthly workers' conference must be maintained by the school. All these will eventuate in better Bible teaching, more soul-winning, and greater co-operation in worldwide missionary endeavor.

III. THE FOURFOLD VALUE OF THE STANDARD OF EXCELLENCE

1. *To Furnish an Incentive for Doing Better Work*

Someone has said, "It is the business of executives to supply incentives." Experience has taught thousands of Sunday school workers that the setting up of the Standard of Excellence before a group of workers as a worthy goal reacts as an immediate and powerful incentive.

Again, the Sunday school, to do its best work, must ever have before it a definite objective. This prevents a Sunday school from going round in a circle. A Sunday school without a goal spends a lot of its time beating the air. There is much lost motion. Its work is haphazard, hit or miss, according to "luck"; it gets nowhere because it is not going anywhere. If a Sunday school will adopt the Standard of Excellence and begin to work toward attaining the ten requirements, it will have a program of good substantial work and a drawing power because of its definite purpose and increased interest.

The fact that a Sunday school has before it a worthy goal and a high ideal which it is trying to reach can but result in the school's doing better work. One may look high and land low, but one can never look low and land high. The value of a high aim is inestimable.

The Standard of Excellence visualizes the work as it is put before the school. It is definite and worth while; it makes an appeal to the members of the school to do their best and in so doing becomes a worth-while incentive to better work.

2. *To Keep the Work of the Sunday School Properly Balanced*

The Standard of Excellence presents to the school a program of work. Each point presents an important phase of Sunday school activity. Instead of the school emphasizing one or two things it finds in the Standard a well-defined program. Many Sunday schools emphasize only the crowd and the collection. A Sunday school that has attained to, or is working toward, the Standard of Excellence takes into account all the essentials of a good Sunday school. The entire membership soon becomes well informed concerning the things which constitute a good Sunday school and cannot be satisfied simply with counting "noses and nickels."

3. *To Guarantee Better Work*

A Sunday school is in better position to do efficient work after becoming Standard than before. Really this is the purpose of having a Standard school—namely, in order that the school may do first-class work. While the receiving of the Standard award is a testimony of good work done, yet the real satisfaction comes not from being recognized as a Standard school, but because of being better able to perform the task the Sunday school is set to do.

Certainly the attainment of this Standard does not mean that the Sunday school has reached its maximum effectiveness, not at all. Nevertheless, the bringing of a Sunday school to the fulfilling of the ten requirements of the Standard will guarantee better work in that school than was done before.

4. *To Promote the Unity of Southern Baptist Sunday School Work and Methods*

First, each one of the states co-operating with the Southern Baptist Convention has a state mission board with a Sunday school department co-operating in exploiting the Standard of Excellence. Connected with these Sunday school departments and the Sunday School Board of the Southern Baptist Convention, there are numbers of men and women on the field advocating the things set out in the Standard of Excellence. In connection with and in addition to these forces there are scores and even hundreds of well-developed leaders scattered throughout the territory who are workers in their own Sunday schools and who from time to time go out on special calls for field work. All of these forces are teaching the things contained in the Standard of Excellence. All of this makes for unity of method and work.

Second, Southern Baptists have seminaries, training schools, and scores of schools and colleges with Sunday school departments—all of them teaching the things incorporated in the Standard of Excellence.

Third, thousands of Sunday schools in the Southern Baptist Convention have on display the large wall chart of the Standard of Excellence. They are striving continuously to meet the requirements and holding the Standard constantly before their members as a goal. Hundreds of schools have met these requirements, many having met them each year for a number of years, and the number is growing rapidly. All these forces back of the Standard of Excellence have done much toward unifying Southern Baptist Sunday school work and methods.

QUESTIONS FOR REVIEW

1. State the design of the Standard of Excellence.
2. Name the ten requirements of the Standard of Excellence.
3. What three things are necessary in building a good Sunday school?
4. What is the twofold aim of the Standard of Excellence?
5. State the fourfold value of the Standard of Excellence.
6. What should be the highest motive prompting a Sunday school to become Standard?

2

CHURCH RELATIONSHIP

Standard requirement:

1. *The church shall elect the officers and teachers.*

2. *The school shall make monthly or quarterly reports to the church.*

The purpose of this requirement is to relate the Sunday school properly to the church. The requirement naturally divides itself into two parts.

I. OFFICERS AND TEACHERS ELECTED BY THE CHURCH

Sunday school work is church work. Sunday school officers and teachers are as truly doing church work when engaged in discharging their duties in the Sunday school as when attending the preaching service or the prayer meeting, or when giving their means to church support and missions.

The Sunday school is the school of the church. The church should elect its officers and teachers—all of them—every officer from the superintendent of the Cradle Roll to the superintendent of the Extension department and every teacher from the Nursery to the Adult classes and every visitor in the Cradle Roll and Extension departments. In the election of the officers and teachers of the Sunday school by the church, the Sunday school is given its proper place as a church school.

1. *Some Advantages of the Church's Electing Officers and Teachers*

Great advantages accrue from making the Sunday school officers and teachers officers of the church.

(1) *Church responsibility for the kind and quality of teaching done in the Sunday school.*—By electing the officers and teachers of the Sunday school the church properly assumes responsibility for what they do and teach. A church is particular, and rightly so, about whom it shall have for pastor. Before calling a man as pastor, it will desire to know many things about him: what kind of man he is, what kind of preacher, and what he believes concerning the Bible and the great fundamental doctrines; and, above all, whether he is God's man for the place. Should the church not be equally concerned about the life, character, knowledge, beliefs, and other spiritual qualifications of the men and women who teach in the Sunday school? It is high time that the churches everywhere were recognizing and assuming this responsibility and electing officers who know how to run the Sunday school and teachers who know what to teach and how to teach. After electing the officers and teachers and putting them in places of honor and responsibility, it should be made plain to them that they are expected to prepare and fit themselves for their great work.

(2) *Church responsibility for the support of the Sunday school.*—The ideal is for the church to finance the Sunday school, providing all the necessary equipment and supplies for the use of officers, teachers, and pupils. This plan contemplates a common treasury for all the organizations of the church, and all the money contributed through the Sunday school will go into this treasury. Likewise, all the needed equipment, supplies, material, and other expenses for the Sunday school will

be paid for out of this treasury. Special Sunday school offerings for missions and benevolences will, of course, go through the church treasury to the causes for which they were given.

This plan puts the church back of the Sunday school financially and gives the Sunday school substantial assurance of the sympathy and unqualified support of the church. Officers, teachers, and classes should not find it necessary to go into their own pockets for money to build and equip the rooms. The building is the property of the church, and it should be equipped for the use of the Sunday school at the expense of the church. The officers and teachers are servants of the church, and the church should provide them with the necessary material and tools with which to do the best work.

Many churches need education along this line, and the pastor can do much to lead the church to adopt a liberal financial policy toward the Sunday school.

(3) *Magnifying the work in the thinking of the workers.*—The officers and teachers represent their church in what they do and teach in the Sunday school, and when they are properly elected by the church and given assurance of the sympathy and financial support of the church, it will make a vast difference in their attitude toward all the activities of the church.

Unconsciously they will feel an obligation to the Sunday school not realized before. The pastor and superintendent can make reasonable requirements of them concerning their regular attendance at the Sunday school, the officers and teachers' meeting, and the workers' conference. And an appeal to them to attend the training classes for better preparation for their work will find a ready response on the part of the majority of workers when they realize that they have been selected by the Holy Spirit and elected by the church for service.

2. *Methods of Electing Officers and Teachers*

In the election of the officers and teachers of the Sunday school incorrect methods shall be avoided:

(1) *Incorrect methods.*—Workers should not be nominated in open church conference. During a business session, the church should not go through the process of selecting and electing its Sunday school officers and teachers one by one. This plan loses sight of the genius of the Sunday school organization.

The entire force should not be re-elected without due consideration. During a church conference at the close of the year, someone should not move that "the present officers and teachers be elected to serve another year." Many churches do it this way, but it will never produce an efficient Sunday school.

The present officers and teachers of the Sunday school should not constitute themselves a nominating committee and nominate the officers and teachers for the ensuing year. This is frequently done, but it is a violation of the principles of democracy and means a self-perpetuating organization, which makes for neither efficiency nor freedom of action.

Neither should the deacons take upon themselves the management of the Sunday school and nominate the officers and teachers. This is not among the prerogatives or duties of the deacons, and it would not be wise for the church to delegate this authority to them in their official capacity.

(2) *Correct method.*—The election sets up the organization to produce growth, or stagnation, during the coming year. It should occur annually, a month to six weeks before the close of the Sunday school year. It should be understood by the officers and teachers that they are elected for only one year, and that their term of office expires at the end of the year for which they

were elected. Those who study the work and attend faithfully to their duties should be re-elected year after year. Those who are unfaithful in the discharge of their duties should be willing to step aside and allow others to take their places at the discretion of the church.

Too often the work has lagged and the cause suffered because an officer or teacher continually neglected his duties, yet held on to his office or class year after year, while fear of giving offense prevented the church from relieving the situation. Literally thousands of Sunday schools are suffering because officers and teachers are willing to accept the honors which go with the positions, but are unable or unwilling to do the work demanded.

If the churches would adopt the policy of electing the officers and teachers annually, and make it clear that their terms are for one year only, it would help greatly to correct this condition. While Sunday school teachers and officers should not be elected for life, yet they should make the Sunday school work their lifework. Of course, where changes are needed, these should be made without hesitation.

The superintendent should be elected first and given ample time to complete the organization and mature plans before the beginning of the year. Usually he is elected in July.

The office of Sunday school superintendent carries with it great responsibility. It should also carry with it corresponding authority. However, it is the authority that goes with leadership rather than that of management.

The superintendent is elected by the church and put in charge of the church's Sunday school. The success of the school is thereby entrusted to him. If the Sunday school is a success, it is because he makes it so. If it is a failure, he cannot shift the responsibility for failure upon the shoulders of others. He alone is responsible. Therefore, he should have every liberty in directing the affairs of the Sunday school; in other words, he should be superintendent of the Sunday school with all that the word *superintendent* means.

He should not be elected for life, but for one year. If his conduct of the affairs of the Sunday school is successful, he should be re-elected each year as long as such is the case. It is not good for a Sunday school to change superintendents often. It requires years to build up a great Sunday school, and frequent changes in leadership are hurtful.

Experience teaches that a nominating committee, appointed by the pastor and composed of three of the wisest and best members of the church, together with the pastor, should carefully and prayerfully go over the entire situation and recommend to the church for election the man who, in its judgment, is best suited for the place of superintendent. When the nominating committee is appointed, the pastor should charge the church to pray that the Holy Spirit may lead the members of the committee in all their deliberations, guiding them to the man whom God would have elected. The Sunday school superintendent should be elected in answer to prayer.

The committee should make its report to the church in conference. The church may reject the recommendation of the nominating committee, but it would rarely do so. The church should elect by a rising vote. The superintendent-elect should be formally presented to the church by the pastor or a member of the committee. Such presentation is not merely formal, it is an expression to the superintendent that the church has confidence in him and authorizes him, in consultation with the pastor, to nominate the other officers and teachers of the Sunday school and otherwise to perfect the organization of the Sunday school and report such action to the church in time for ratification or modification by the beginning of the new year.

Let the superintendent lead in selecting the other officers and teachers. The newly elected superintendent and the pastor should make a careful review of the work of all the officers and teachers during the past year. There may be a need to transfer certain workers from one position to another. This, of course, ought to be done wisely.

A careful study of the church membership should be made, and new officers and teachers should be added to the organization each year. After thorough agreement has been reached as to who should constitute the teaching forces for the next year, the superintendent and pastor should interview personally each one chosen for service and secure his consent to teach or work in whatever capacity he is needed. The superintendent should nominate at a church conference those who have been selected for the respective positions. The church ought to elect by a rising vote. If practical, the pastor should use the Sunday school for his Sunday morning theme and present the officers and teachers to the congregation, which should give them a rising vote of confidence and assurance of loyal support.

In the event that the Sunday school is departmentized, the general superintendent and the pastor should select and enlist the department superintendents. The matter of selecting and enlisting the other department officers and teachers should be placed upon the superintendent of each department. The department superintendents should always co-operate with the general superintendent and the pastor by securing their consent before a prospective worker is approached for any department. No one should be asked to serve in any department except by previous agreement of the general superintendent, pastor, and department superintendent. This applies to substitute teachers also.

3. *Resignations*

In the event that it becomes necessary at any time for the general superintendent to resign for any cause whatever, he should hand his resignation to the church, and the church would take whatever action is desired.

Should it become necessary for any other general officer or department superintendent of the Sunday school to resign, he should hand his resignation to the superintendent who, with the pastor, would give it due consideration.

Should any other department officer or teacher find it necessary to resign, he should hand his resignation to the superintendent of the department in which he works, who, with the general superintendent and the pastor, would consider the matter. Where there are no department heads, all resignations should go to the general superintendent.

II. The Sunday School Making Reports to the Church

The superintendent of the school should submit a written report of the work of the school to the church. He should give account of his stewardship. This will help in many ways and should be carefully and skilfully done.

1. *Values Inherent in Making Reports*

There are certain values inherent in the making of these reports to the church that should challenge the superintendent to plan painstakingly to make the most of such opportunities.

(1) *An incentive to the officers and teachers.*—Reporting the work of the Sunday school regularly to the church will help the Sunday school officers and teachers to realize that they are representing their church, and will greatly enhance the importance of the work in their thinking, thus causing them to strive earnestly to fulfil this obligation to the best of their abilities.

(2) *An opportunity to place the work of the school definitely before the church.*—The pastor and the superintendent, by reporting on the Sunday school work, will have opportunities each month to call the attention of the church membership to the good work the Sunday school is doing and to urge every church member to participate in the Bible teaching service of the church.

(3) *An occasion to commend good work publicly.*—Flattery should never be used but the honest and sincere recognition of good work done is deserved and becomes both a means of encouragement and an incentive. The pastor and superintendent should take advantage of the opportunity thus afforded to commend publicly the work of deserving individuals and groups.

2. *Methods of Presenting Reports*

Reports should be illuminating. In addition to showing the church the standing of the school, they should be made in such a manner as to stir the members of the Sunday school greatly and encourage them to further endeavor.

Comparative reports are most effective. If progress is being made, it is an incentive to yet greater effort; if reports show a decline, prompt action may be taken at once to remedy the situation.

If possible, the report of the entire Sunday school by departments and classes should be multigraphed or printed and distributed to the congregation at the preaching service. This will inspire the school and arouse enthusiasm. Only such items should be reported as will be of general interest. Usually people are interested in the attendance, offering, number of pupils joining the church, and number of pupils baptized. However, the items receiving special note, as a rule, should be determined by the work that is being done. Such a report may be made through the church bulletin on the first Sunday morning in each month.

The superintendent should present a digest of this report to the church in its monthly business meeting, which report should be filed by the church clerk.

The monthly report for the church in conference and for the files of the church clerk should be made out on Six Point Record Form 135 (available from Baptist Book Store).

QUESTIONS FOR REVIEW

1. Mention three advantages of the church's electing officers and teachers.

2. Discuss the ideal plan for financing the Sunday school.

3. Discuss the best method of electing the superintendent; the other officers and teachers.

4. Give three values inherent in making reports to the church.

5. How should these reports be made to the church?

ENLARGEMENT

Standard requirement:

1. *The enrolment of the school shall at least equal the number of resident church members as recognized by the church.*

2. *The school shall promote a program of visitation.*

In checking on this requirement the first necessary information is the recognized *resident* church membership (not the total reported membership). To meet this requirement, the Sunday school enrolment, including the Cradle Roll and Extension departments, the general and department officers and teachers, shall at least be equal to the number of resident church members.

This is the only one of the ten requirements in the Standard of Excellence that refers directly to the subject of Sunday school enlargement. The other nine requirements deal with the school's efficiency; that is, with what the school should do for the pupil after he becomes a member.

Development in Sunday school growth is not confined to any particular locality or section of the country nor to any special types of Sunday schools. Rural churches, town churches, and city churches, both in "down-town" and residential sections, can experience a material increase in enrolment and in attendance when right methods of Sunday school building are employed.

Note a few examples:

A Sunday school in a country community had for years maintained an attendance of about sixty. It was graded and moved up from a class to a department pattern and at once began to grow and in a few months had a regular attendance of about two hundred.

A Sunday school in a small town, having a regular attendance of fifty, as a result of a training school culminating in a census, moved up to a department pattern. It began to take on new life and within a year was having a regular attendance of about three hundred.

A Sunday school in a large city had for twenty-five years maintained an attendance of around four hundred. Some proved, up-to-date methods were employed and within eighteen months the school was having a regular attendance of 1,500.

The explanation: *Vision, Study, Right Methods, and Work.*

Pastors and superintendents are fast realizing that we have just been playing at the Sunday school business from the standpoint of reaching people, and that a large Sunday school can be built wherever people live in large numbers.

There is inspiration in numbers, but let it be understood that a school does not necessarily have to have an enrolment of a thousand members to be great. It may be a really great school and have an attendance of a hundred or even less. However, no Sunday school is worthy of being called a great school unless it is reaching a large majority of the people who should attend it. This is true no matter what other claims to efficiency it may have.

The Standard of Excellence emphasizes this as a great principle underlying Sunday school work, and requires that a Sunday school must be reaching the people in a large way before being entitled to recognition as a Standard school.

The requirement that a Sunday school must have on its rolls a number equal to the resident church membership is not a difficult requirement. There is no good reason for a Sunday school anywhere not being able to meet this requirement if the proper methods are used.

I. THE CONSTITUENCY FOR THE SUNDAY SCHOOL SHOULD BE KNOWN

The constituency of the Sunday school can be secured from three sources, namely, the present Sunday school roll, the church roll, and the prospects found by taking a religious census of the community.

1. *Checking the Church Membership Roll*

Certainly every church member should be in Sunday school. Every church member should be studying the Bible. He should be studying the Bible with the other church members in the Sunday school. There is little definite Bible study done outside of the Sunday school, not enough to take into consideration, so we might say that people who do not go to Sunday school do not study the Bible.

The first source from which we begin building the attendance of the Sunday school is the membership of the church—the members should be in the Sunday school. Let the superintendent and pastor go carefully over the church roll, compare it with the Sunday school roll, and make a list of all those who do not attend the Sunday school.

2. *Taking A Religious Census*

A religious census should be taken at least annually in every community; in growing centers and communities, twice each year; and in mill and factory districts, with shifting, changing populations, a canvass may be needed every three months. The purpose of the census is to get information to be used in building the Sunday school. At the same time, it is a good way and worth while to let the people know that the Sunday school is at work and anxious to help in every way possible.

Either the pastor or the general superintendent should take charge and act as general director of the census, or some definite individual should be selected and enlisted for this work. The following steps should be taken to guarantee a successful house-to-house canvass and to make this work most effective.

(1) *Defining the territory.*—The legitimate territory for which the church is responsible should be decided upon by the superintendent and pastor and any others they wish to consult. A specific definition of this territory will need to be given for the census. In cities, maps may be used and certain boundary streets or natural divisions can be found. In rural communities roads will serve.

(2) *Preparing the assignments.*—The preparation of the territory for assignment will need careful clerical attention by some who are familiar with it. There should be the general division into some four or more districts, according to size, using natural or assigned dividing lines. If possible, have a good map of each district. Then each one of these districts should be subdivided into blocks or sections small enough to be canvassed by a worker in two hours' time. The number of these small divisions will, of course, determine how many census takers must be enlisted.

Each block or section should indicate how many houses are contained in it. Use a card, or secure an envelope for this purpose large enough to hold the census cards and draw an outline map of the territory on the front of the envelope. These envelopes may be secured from your Baptist Book Store. Follow the same general plan in towns and rural communities, using the natural dividing lines, roads, highways, etc., in preparing the territory.

(3) *Enlisting the workers.*—A capable individual should be selected and placed in charge of each of the larger districts as captain. His task would be to familiarize himself with his territory and at the proper time, when his workers are assigned to him, be ready quickly to assign the territory to them, get them out on the field, and assist them in any other way possible. He should not be responsible for enlisting the workers.

Then comes the task of actually enlisting the necessary census takers. One fine way is to assign a quota to each department, and, in the Young People's and Adult ages, to each class. Then lead them to work toward getting the quota actually signed on the dotted line at least one week before the census is to be taken.

Each age group up through the Juniors should be asked for a quota equalling the number of officers and teachers. The fifteen- and sixteen-year-old Intermediates make fine workers if paired off with Adults.

The pastor will lay it upon the hearts of the people from the pulpit and the superintendent will do the same from the platform, but the task of securing the workers to do the canvassing must be done by personal solicitation, and urging will often be necessary. No effort should go unused and no slackening of energy should be allowed until sufficient census takers have been secured.

(4) *Providing sufficient materials.*—Many times the taking of a census is handicapped because of insufficient materials with which to work.

There should be a most liberal supply of census cards. Every home is to be entered and a card filled out for every individual. A shortage of materials here will prove disastrous. For the best results, do not change the card. The simpler it is and the fewer questions it carries, the easier will be the work and the more nearly complete the information secured.

Other materials will include a sufficient supply of pencils, rubber bands, and the census assignment envelopes carrying "Instructions to Census Takers."

(5) *Selecting the time and instructing the workers.*— Any season of the year is suitable, and any time a good time for this work. The best day in the week for the work in most cases is Sunday afternoon. It is the most suitable time as the people are at leisure and it is easier to get the required number of census takers.

In this day of Sunday afternoon outings it is far better to arrange to serve a light lunch in the church at the close of the morning service and send the census takers out by one o'clock. This will increase the effectiveness of the census at least a third. Otherwise, gather at the church as early in the afternoon as possible.

At the appointed hour gather the census takers together for a period of devotion and general instruction. Give each census taker a copy of "Instructions to Census Takers." These instructions are on the back of the census assignment envelope, Form 680. These may be ordered from your Baptist Book Store.

Three things will need especial emphasis at this meeting: First, let it be thoroughly understood that the workers must go into every home where white people live, talk with the people no matter who they are and get information concerning everybody. Second, insist that a card should be made for each individual in the home. No one is to be omitted and no two are to be combined on one card. Third, make clear that every blank is to be filled. If any question is not answered the card may possibly have to be thrown away. Workers should not be allowed to take the census unless they attend the meeting for instructions, for they cannot be counted on nor expected to know how to do this work correctly and efficiently.

(6) *Assigning the territory.*—The general instructions ought not to occupy more than fifteen minutes. The meeting should then break up into sections which should be presided over by the district captains, who should quickly assign to each worker the territory he is to canvass. Each captain should have a secretary to list the workers as they are assigned their territory and to see that each one is provided with a pencil and a liberal supply of census cards. Also each captain should have enough automobiles to send his workers out to their territory. Instruct them to bring all the cards back to the church as soon as their work is completed.

It is most helpful for the pastor at the Sunday evening preaching service to give a few minutes for verbal reports from the workers. Many short, helpful sermons will come out of their experiences.

3. Preparing the Information for Use

The information as brought by the census takers and secured from the church roll is not by any means ready to be used, and little lasting good will come from the work done unless it is put in convenient form to be used.

(1) *Assorting the information.*—All cards showing a preference for other denominations are thrown to themselves. All the other information would belong to the church taking the census. Included in this would be the membership of the church taking the census, all the members of their families, Baptists with membership else-

where, persons expressing preference for Baptist churches, and all those expressing no preference. All this information should be carefully checked against the church and Sunday school rolls so that a composite of the three sources of information will be available and so that duplications can be eliminated.

(2) *Grading the information.*—The next step is to grade all the information gained from the church roll and the census. This should be done on the age group basis, as follows:

Cradle Roll and Nursery—birth through 3
Beginners—4, 5
Primaries—6, 7, 8
Juniors—9, 10, 11, 12
Intermediates—13, 14, 15, 16
Young People—17 through 24
Adults—25 and above
Extension—all who cannot attend Sunday school

All above eight years of age should be graded by sex as well as by age.

Where the possibilities for a Sunday school are large, the information will have to be graded closely. Often provision will have to be made for one or more departments for each age below Young People's, with several classes for each age of boys and each age of girls in the Junior and Intermediate departments. In such cases there should be close grading for all Young People and Adults also. Separate classes and departments should be provided for married Young People. The information would determine how many classes there ought to be in each department. The classes for Beginners, Primaries, Juniors, and Intermediates should be kept small, not more than ten to each class, and even smaller.

(3) *Tabulating the information.*—The next thing after grading the information is to tabulate it. It should be

typewritten and visitation assignments should be prepared. This is absolutely necessary if the best results are to be had. The census cards may be used as the basis for a permanent prospect file.

It is best, if the information is typewritten, to have at least five copies made, one each for the pastor, superintendent, department superintendent, and teacher, and one to be filed for future reference. Some schools have the information printed or mimeographed in order that each member may be furnished with a copy. In this way it is easier to keep a permanent record of the possibilities for the school.

It is well for a school to supplement these lists by assigning a few prospects to each teacher each week, with the understanding that they are to be visited by the class within the week. Reports of the visits will be turned in at the weekly officers and teachers' meeting.

II. The Organization Should Be Enlarged

It will be necessary to enlarge the organization in order to take care of all the people on the church roll and those discovered in the census. There will be no use to go on with the same old organization hoping to increase the size of the Sunday school permanently. Unless the present Sunday school organization is enlarged, practically all of the work done in taking the census will come to naught.

To be sure, a few people will join the Sunday school as a result of being visited during the census, but there can be no large permanent growth unless there is an organization strong enough to reach, hold, and teach the people who should be in the Sunday school. A church should provide at least one worker for every ten people it seeks to enrol in its Sunday school. The size of the organization needed is dictated by the number of pupils available, as revealed by the information secured.

Immediately this organization should be outlined and the leaders should set themselves to the enlistment of the necessary workers. Where will a Sunday school look for so many additional teachers? How will they be induced to take up the work? They are to be found within the membership of the church and nowhere else. If approached in the right manner they can be induced to serve. There are three steps which, if followed persistently, will produce the required number of officers and teachers:

1. *Praying Publicly and Privately for Workers*

Prayer is a proved method; Jesus used it. He prayed all night before choosing the twelve apostles. He commanded us to use it. He said, "Pray ye therefore the Lord of the harvest, that he will send forth labourers into his harvest" (Matt: 9:38).

The task of choosing and enlisting these new officers and teachers for the Sunday school should be made a matter of prayer at all services. It should be made a subject of private prayer daily by the pastor, the superintendent, and all others who are interested. There is no undertaking which requires greater faith and more wisdom than this. (James 1:5-7)

2. *Making a List of Prospective Officers and Teachers*

The pastor and superintendent should carefully go over the church roll, name by name, and make a list of all the members possessing teaching gifts and qualities of leadership. A study of the church membership from this viewpoint will be illuminating and encouraging.

As the superintendent and pastor select from the church roll those who possess teaching gifts and qualifications, they should write their names into the new organization, adjusting each one to the place in which he is best suited to serve. Changes and readjustments will be necessary before the new organization is completed. Many delightful thrills will come to the pastor and superintendent as they study the church membership with reference to the ability of each one to serve in the Sunday school in some capacity.

3. *Securing the Consent of Those Who Have Been Selected to Serve*

It is surprising how men and women who love God will respond to a definite appeal to service. Many of the best men and women in all churches have done little in Christian service because they have never been offered an appealing task. To the question, "Why stand ye here all the day idle?" the answer comes back, "No man hath hired us." "We have no task—we do not know what to do."

The superintendent and pastor should hold personal interviews with all those who have been selected to serve, and urge them to accept the work assigned them. Visualize the task to all, lay it heavily upon their hearts and pray with them and for them. Show that man a list of eight boys fourteen years of age who need him to go after them and teach them and win them to Christ. Show that young woman seven girls ten years of age who need her—many of them not in the Sunday school, and perhaps not one of them knowing Christ. Do not take "no" for an answer. Be insistent. No Christian should allow any pretext to turn him aside, such as lack of time, pressing household duties, and similar age-old excuses.

There are many capable young people in all the churches who love the Lord and really desire to serve him. They may be frivolous and gay and even worldly. Go after them. Lay upon their hearts their obligation to serve Christ. Win them away from the things they are doing by giving them a place where they may serve Christ. Do not give up. Get the teachers.

When they answer that they do not know how to teach, promise to give them the necessary help. This book and other books of the Sunday School Training Course should be put into the hands of each one of them. A training class should be organized and they should be led in a study of the book selected. The pastor, the superintendent, or someone else capable of doing so should teach this class. A functioning weekly officers and teachers' meeting will offer effective in-service training. Find the teachers, enlist them, and train them.

III. A Suitable Place Should Be Provided

There is no such thing as building a Sunday school great in numbers in small, cramped quarters. Neither can a Sunday school of the highest efficiency be operated without proper equipment. While good equipment does not necessarily guarantee an efficient Sunday school, at the same time, it is necessary if a Sunday school is to do the best quality of work.

1. *Adjusting Present Quarters*

In planning to increase the growth of the Sunday school, it is often necessary to readjust the arrangements of the building. Often an Adult class is meeting in a large room when a much smaller room would serve its purpose. If properly approached the class can easily be induced to make the exchange and the large room may be utilized for taking care of an entire department with small classes. Other rooms may sometimes be divided by sound-proof partitions in such a way as to provide for more classes so that the teachers may work with greater effectiveness.

Frequently there is not half room enough in the present quarters. As a temporary arrangement it is sometimes wise to secure outside space. Perhaps a lodge room may be secured close by for the Junior or Intermediate department or for an Adult class. A public school building near by may be rented for one or more classes or entire departments. A tabernacle may be erected close by the church building to take care of one or more departments or one or more classes.

Again let it be said that a large Sunday school cannot be built and maintained in small, cramped quarters; and sane, sensible arrangements should be made for the expansion of the Sunday school. The building fixes the pattern for the Sunday school, sometimes for years to come.

2. *Erecting New Buildings*

Many Sunday schools have to "swarm" before the church membership realizes that a larger, better equipped building is needed. Hundreds and even thousands of our church houses in the Southern Baptist Convention territory are wholly inadequate from the standpoint of size and proper adjustment to take care of the Sunday schools the churches should have. In many of these situations, churches should erect new buildings, both from the standpoint of efficiency and economy. There is no economy in a church maintaining a small, inefficient Sunday school when there are multitudes of people all around who could be won if adequate quarters were provided. A church that takes care of its home base, all things being equal, will do more in the way of giving the gospel to those afar. The command from our Saviour is, "Ye shall be witnesses unto me both in Jerusalem, and in all Judaea, and in Samaria, and unto the uttermost part of the earth."

IV. THE ENLARGED ORGANIZATION SHOULD BE SET UP

The Sunday following the religious census the new enlarged organization should be put into operation. The simplest and easiest way to do this is to grade the present Sunday school and assign the teachers to the pupils present; then put into the hands of the teacher of each class a list of all the pupils for whom he is responsible. Be sure no name is omitted. List all the pupils who are enrolled, plus all the prospective pupils secured from the church roll and discovered in the census.

Grading the Sunday school should be adopted by the church as its policy. It should receive the loyal support of all the officers and teachers. The reasons for grading should be made clear to all. When people have been properly prepared, it is easy to set up the needed departments and classes, with a clearly defined age range for each. In every age group, Adults included, Baptists have proved themselves ready to co-operate fully when they are led to understand the reasons for grading.

If the Six Point Record System is to be installed, a new classification of the entire school should be made, but care must be taken that no name is lost from the Sunday school roll.

When the new organization is set up, many teachers will have small classes to begin with, and perhaps some will not have any pupils at all. There should be placed in each teacher's hand the names of a sufficient number of prospective pupils to make a class when they are brought into the Sunday school. This is the condition which sends workers afield and produces Sunday school growth.

V. A PROGRAM OF VISITATION SHOULD BE MAINTAINED

The visitation of prospects and absentees is absolutely essential to the growth of any Sunday school. This is the last step in reaching the people and in constantly building up the membership and attendance of a Sunday school.

1. *A Program of Visitation*

As the matter now stands, during the enlargement campaign:

The church roll has been checked.

The census has been taken.

The information has been assorted, graded, and tabulated.

The organization has been enlarged to take care of all the possibilities.

The enlarged organization has been inaugurated.

The proper space has been provided in the building.

The information has been placed in the hands of the officers and teachers.

If we stop here, all the work which has been done will be largely in vain, the organization will go to pieces and discouragement will result on every hand.

The thing needed now to enlarge the Sunday school membership is that this organization should be led by the superintendent and pastor to visit every one of the prospective pupils during the coming week and urge them to come to the Sunday school, and then keep visiting them from week to week with the same urgent invitation until all of them join.

At all times a sharp lookout for new pupils should be maintained by the heads of the departments, teachers, and pupils. All people moving into the community during the year should be located and visited as soon after their arrival as possible, and their names should be reported to the pastor and superintendent. The department superintendents and the class officers should be on the alert, going after the newcomers continually for their departments and classes.

As the Sunday school roll increases, the absentee list will also increase and it will be necessary for teachers and officers to visit absent pupils regularly week by week if they are to build them up in regular attendance.

Thus the visitation ministry of a school will assume large proportions and will demand constant attention. Regular weekly visitation should be accomplished, the assignments being made and the reports received at the weekly officers and teachers' meeting. Special visitation times should be fostered for different groups. Individual visitation should be continuously urged and assignments made. All the ingenuity, skill and consecration of the leaders will be needed to plan a varied visitation program and inspire the workers constantly to participate in this all-important work. A definite plan of visitation is heartily recommended for all Sunday schools.

2. *A Regular Visitation Day*

If the best results are to come, a regular weekly or monthly visitation day should be observed. The main purpose of such a day is to visit the prospective pupils and to contact absentees.

(1) *The purpose of visitation day.*—The purpose of a regular visitation day is: First, to visit and urge all absent pupils to come back to the Sunday school; second, to visit the prospective pupils who have been discovered and urge them to become members of the Sunday school; third, to keep on the lookout for people moving into the community, locate them as soon after their arrival as possible, and report their names to the pastor and the superintendent.

A regular visitation day prayerfully and intelligently observed is almost a sure method of getting in touch with newcomers and will result in the return of absent pupils to the Sunday school. Often the list of prospective pupils secured in the census will be thoroughly worked up within a short time. A live list of prospective pupils may be secured for all the departments and classes by maintaining a well-planned and well-executed visitation day.

(2) *The best time to observe visitation day.*—In most cases Thursday is a satisfactory time for visitation day. It may be well to have the visitation for some age groups done during the day. Other age groups may be more effectively visited at night. A definite schedule should be set up and followed.

It is impossible to get a time that will suit and please all, but in the great majority of city and town schools, people can easily spend an hour or two regularly once a week visiting for the Lord. To be sure, some of the people will have to work and cannot go. However, if the matter is properly presented, it will be possible to get one or more representatives from each class to take part in the visitation.

Some Sunday schools select Saturday afternoon because it is a half holiday and the people in cities who work in offices, factories, shops, and other like places are at leisure, and are usually glad to give an hour to visiting. Again, Saturday afternoon has the advantage of proximity to Sunday, and may yield better results on this account.

Agree to have a regular visitation day, set a time for it, plan for it, observe it.

(3) *The plan for visitation day.*—Someone asked, "Why have a specified visitation day? Why not everybody visit when he can?" That is the very reason for setting aside a definite time to do Sunday school visiting. "Everybody" doesn't visit "when he can." Remember this, people who do Sunday school visiting only when it is convenient, do not visit at all.

The value of having a plan for Sunday school visiting lies largely in the fact that people will visit in groups and not alone. For this reason the Sunday school ought to agree to have a regular visitation day, select the time that will suit the largest number, and observe it. The pastor should make frequent references to it from the pulpit and it should be given as much publicity as possible.

The direction of the whole matter necessarily should be in the hands of the general superintendent. He should be the guiding spirit and see to it that the day is planned for regularly. However, the planning and visiting can be done best by departments. Each department superintendent would naturally direct the work of visiting in his department. He can do whatever planning is necessary with his teachers at the weekly officers and teachers' meeting. Of course, each teacher should also visit his own pupils and prospects at other times.

Nothing should be left to chance. A sufficient number of automobiles should be secured and the routings of each arranged. Promptly at the specified time all who are to engage in the visitation should meet at the church building. The department superintendents should quickly get their officers and teachers together and assign them their visiting lists and send them out with as little delay as possible.

First, every pupil who was absent the previous Sunday should be visited and earnestly urged to be in his place the following Sunday.

Second, group leaders should plan with their group members to visit their absentees and the one or two prospects assigned to the group.

Third, every teacher should have a list of prospective pupils who should be visited and lovingly invited to join the Sunday school.

The Six Point Record System offers forms for making visitation assignments and reporting the results. The use of these forms will point out the purpose of the visit and so help train the visitors. Making a report in writing serves to keep the information in the church files up to date. It also trains the visitor to summarize and evaluate his visit and often furnishes an incentive for a further visit.

(4) *The ones who should do the visiting.*—The pastor and superintendent should frequently go. Usually they would be on the lookout for new teachers; they should also call on the sick and those in trouble. If for no other reason, they should go for the influence of their example.

The department superintendents should lead the teachers and pupils in their departments, being sure that no one is overlooked who should be visited. Sometimes a department superintendent may have to do the visiting for one or more of his teachers who could not possibly go. Often he will visit with an inexperienced teacher.

Every teacher who can possibly arrange to go should avail himself of the opportunity offered by visitation day to visit his absent pupils. He should also gain new recruits for his class from the list of prospects furnished him. This is the teacher's best chance to build the class.

Group leaders of Young People's and Adult classes should enlist their groups to join enthusiastically in this campaign. They should go in groups under the direction of the group leader.

Junior and Intermediate pupils will be glad to join their teachers and will enjoy greatly the work of visiting. A regular visitation day offers an opportunity to Intermediate and Junior teachers to utilize and interest their pupils and enlist them in real service.

A teacher of an Intermediate class of girls had the regular members of her class meet at her home and go to the church in a body. One of the girls was heard to remark that she was "just crazy about Sunday school visiting."

Several members of a class of Intermediate boys of ten members, not one of whom had been absent for a month, met, at the suggestion of their teacher, and helped other classes with their visitation.

The Cradle Roll superintendent and her workers will find the regular visitation day a delightful time to visit in the interest of the Cradle Roll. Birthday cards and other materials can be delivered to the homes and many new babies enrolled in the Cradle Roll department.

The Extension department superintendent and visitors can also take advantage of this opportunity, delivering literature and looking out for new members for this department.

(5) *The benefits of a regular visitation day.*—The Sunday school will grow in numbers. This is certain. The one unfailing method of reaching new pupils for the Sunday school and bringing back the absentees is the personal visit. People will join the Sunday school if they are asked. It is not nearly so difficult to reach people for the Sunday school as we imagine. It is far more difficult to get members of the Sunday school to visit them. The absentee list of any Sunday school can be reduced by fifty to seventy-five per cent if the absentees are contacted each week and sufficiently urged to return to the school.

Through visitation the officers and teachers of the Sunday school come into personal touch with the pupils in their homes and places of business, and they can thus plan the more intelligently to meet their needs. Often the co-operation of parents is secured in this way and a correct solution of the problems confronting many of the pupils reached. On the other hand, when the parents of pupils are totally indifferent to their spiritual well-being, a knowledge of this condition will help the teacher in meeting his pupils' needs.

The pastor gains valuable information of his entire field through the Sunday school officers and teachers. The visitors should make written reports to the pastor of all cases really needing his attention.

The teachers have an opportunity to enlist their pupils in definite service. Both teachers and pupils will become more intensely interested in the school and in other people as they experience the joys which come through visiting. As they carry blessings into the homes and lives of those whom they visit, they too are blessed.

The Sunday school will be supplied with new material for building the school. New people moving into the community are quickly discovered by the visitors. The annual census is not sufficient, as in growing towns and centers people are moving in all during the year.

Going after people personally is the one unfailing method of reaching them for the Sunday school. Jesus gave us this method of how to get people into the Sunday school in the parable of the supper in the fourteenth chapter of Luke: "The master of the house . . . said to his servant, . . . Go out into the highways and hedges, and compel them to come in, that my house may be filled."

This method of going after people was good two thousand years ago and is just as good today. It is good in the city and good in the country. It gets results everywhere, every time. All other methods of reaching people for the Sunday school grow old and ineffective. This method of going after people personally never grows old, but is ever new, attractive, and resultful.

QUESTIONS FOR REVIEW

1. Mention the first step in reaching the people for the Sunday school. From what sources may the information be secured?

2. Why should the Sunday school organization be enlarged?

3. Give three steps necessary in securing the needed number of officers and teachers.

4. What should be done to provide additional room for the enlarged organization?

5. What is the next step in conserving what has been done? Name at least three methods for doing this.

6. State the threefold purpose of a regular visitation day. What is the plan for visitation day?

4

GRADING

Standard requirement:

The school shall be graded as follows: Cradle Roll, birth through 3; Beginners, 4-5; Primaries, 6-8; Juniors, 9-12; Intermediates, 13-16; Young People, 17-24; Adults, 25 and above; and an Extension department for those who cannot attend.

(Note.—If possible, one or more Nurseries should be provided for children, birth through three.)

The question of grading the Sunday school is an old one. It is in many respects the most important question which confronts Sunday school workers today. The reason for this is that if a Sunday school is properly graded, it is possible to have everything else of value needed to make the Sunday school efficient.

The day of the ungraded Sunday school is long past. Today it is the fashion for progressive Sunday schools everywhere to organize on the department pattern.

In considering the matter of grading a Sunday school, it is well to realize that there must be a single basis for grading. Some would grade on scholastic attainment, some according to various ideas of congeniality, and some even according to social relationships. Others would use a mixture of methods. But only a brief consideration is necessary to see that if a school is to be graded there can be only one basis used, for the introduction of more than one basis would immediately produce an ungraded school. This is true of all schools.

I. The Correct Basis for Grading

It is agreed that the Sunday school in its organizations and work should meet the fourfold need of the pupil—the physical, mental, social, and spiritual. However, the first three of these needs are taken into account for one purpose only—namely, to meet the fourth, which is the spiritual need. It is therefore seen that the Sunday school exists for the purpose of meeting the spiritual need of the pupil.

As pupils of the same age have generally the same spiritual needs, it is readily apparent that the true basis for grading in the Sunday school is the pupil's age.

It is not the business of the Sunday school to teach a great mass of facts, not even Bible facts, but great spiritual truths. Facts are only incidental. The ability of the pupil to comprehend a spiritual truth is not based on his ability to understand geography, history, mathematics, Latin, or any of the sciences. The brightest people are by no means always the most spiritually minded, either among children or grown people.

It is perhaps true that the poorest way to grade a Sunday school class for imparting spiritual instruction is on the basis of scholarship. For example, here are two young men twenty years of age; one of them has had only one year of high school work, the other is a college graduate. Both are Christians, or perhaps both are unconverted. It would be unthinkable to separate these two young men in Sunday school classes because of the difference in their mental attainment. Of course, they belong in the same class and are perfectly congenial socially, and certainly their spiritual needs are similar.

Another thing, it is not fair to pupils of an average grade of intelligence to put them into classes with younger pupils because the younger pupils have brighter minds or are further advanced in their secular school work. It is not fair to the advanced pupil to be put with others older than he, nor to one who is small for his age to be with younger pupils.

Such exceptions are unnecessary. The average boy or girl, man or woman, can do all the study required in the Sunday school, using either the Graded or Uniform Lessons. We are on safe pedagogical, theological, and common sense grounds when we adhere strictly to the age basis in grading the Sunday school. On this basis one can also know when his Sunday school is graded, and this is not possible when other methods are used.

II. The Reasons for Grading

There are many reasons for grading a Sunday school. Let us briefly consider three:

1. *To Make It Easier to Reach Those Who Ought to Be in the Sunday School*

If the Sunday school is graded on the age basis, definite responsibility is fixed on certain ones for bringing into the school those who should attend. Take, for example, one Junior department which is responsible for reaching all the boys and girls in the community nine to twelve years of age who ought to be in the Sunday school. The entire organization of the Junior department is made responsible for all these boys and girls. The superintendent of the department would have the greatest responsibility. Next in responsibility are the teachers, each of whom is responsible for reaching every pupil of the age and sex of his class. Grading in the Sunday school creates a condition whereby people can be reached in large numbers for the school.

In order to build a great Sunday school and reach the multitudes who ought to be in Sunday school, it is necessary to grade the entire school, and grade it on the age basis. For only by grading all the age groups can responsibility be definitely placed for reaching the people in the community.

2. *To Make It Easier to Teach Those Who Are in the Sunday School*

The teacher's task should be made as simple and easy as possible by providing for him a Sunday school class composed of pupils of the same age. Certainly no one will dispute this. The Sunday school teacher who really does effective teaching must necessarily know many things about his pupils. For one thing, he must know the general characteristics as determined by the pupil's age.

It is noticeable in Sunday schools that are closely graded on the age basis that the number assigned to each teacher is small, especially up through the Intermediate ages. More and more, the same principle is being applied to Young People and Adults. This is as it should be. Teachers in these departments should have small classes if they wish to do their best work.

Happy is that Sunday school teacher who teaches a small class, say five to seven boys or girls, of the same age! Such a class is in itself a task commensurate with the ability and the time of most teachers; and such teachers can know the pupils and really teach them.

The Sunday school lessons are prepared for pupils on the basis of their age. They are adapted to meet the needs of the pupils as they advance year by year. This is true of both the Graded Lessons and the present Uniform Lessons. They are designed for pupils classified with April 1 as the dividing date. Schools which adhere to this date in all their grading get the greatest benefit from the Sunday school lessons helps.

It must ever be borne in mind that a Sunday school teacher must know not only the pupil and the lesson, but also how to teach the lesson to the pupil. Certainly the teacher's task is simplified if he has before him the pupils for whom the lesson was made.

Although there may be a difference in the mental attainment of pupils of the same age in the same Sunday school class, this does not make it ineffective to use the lesson made for pupils of that age. The pupils are substantially alike physically, socially, and spiritually. They have interest in the same things. They have the same spiritual needs. And, comparatively speaking, the task of the teacher is a simple one.

3. *To Make Some Individual Definitely Responsible for Winning Each Lost Pupil to Christ*

Grading fixes responsibility and really makes evangelism practical and effective in the Sunday school. It simply means, for example, that the teacher of fourteen-year-old boys is responsible for winning to Christ all the fourteen-year-old boys in the Sunday school and on the prospect lists for the school. All the unconverted boys fourteen years of age should form this teacher's prayer list. Each one should be on his heart; each one should be definitely looked after and sought for Christ by him.

In this way the pastor and the superintendent have a definite knowledge of all lost people in the Sunday school, and have as co-workers in winning them to Christ teachers definitely charged with the winning of each one. This systematizes the soul-winning work in the church and no lost person in the community is neglected.

III. The Difficulties in the Way of Grading

The majority of our Sunday schools are not really graded. Of course, there are many difficulties, some of which are real and some of which are just imaginary.

1. *Real Difficulties*

The real difficulties in grading a Sunday school lie with the leadership. This is a severe thing to say, but, in the spirit of love, we must recognize where responsibility rests.

Sometimes the officers and teachers do not understand that it is much easier to conduct a graded Sunday school; that a teacher can do far better work in a graded Sunday school; that it is easier to reach the people and bring them into a graded Sunday school; that it is impossible to adjust properly an ungraded Sunday school to any kind of building, and that it is a simple matter to construct and equip a building for a graded school. They do not understand that an ungraded Sunday school can never reach and minister to every member of every family. If the pastors, superintendents, and teachers understood these things it would be but a short time until all our Sunday schools would be graded.

Another serious obstacle in the way of grading is the desire of many teachers to keep their present pupils. The advantages of having the Sunday school graded should be explained and, if possible, all such teachers should be induced to fall in line and co-operate. Otherwise, confusion and discouragement will result.

The superintendent and pastor are often overcautious. They hesitate to step in and disarrange an old organization that is doing fairly well, preferring to "let well enough alone." They are convinced that the Sunday school should be graded, yet, because of the personal preference of this teacher and that teacher, and because it means the inauguration of a new order of things, the breaking up of old ties in dividing classes and adjusting teachers to new tasks, the overcautious pastor and superintendent prefer to let the Sunday school "rock along" as it is.

2. *Imaginary Difficulties*

Sometimes the following difficulties appear to be real, but they are not:

Frequently it is claimed that there are not enough workers, but this is not really the case. True, many more teachers are needed for a graded Sunday school than for a school that is ungraded. After a religious census of the community has been taken the church may realize a need to double or treble the number of workers. The pastor and superintendent will sometimes say, "We haven't enough workers to grade our Sunday school." This is an imaginary difficulty, for every church has within its membership enough teachers and officers to take care of the Sunday school situation. To be sure they are not trained and efficient, but they have been saved and they are good raw material out of which fine officers and teachers can be made. They need to be trained and put to work in the Sunday school.

There are enough teachers and officers for all the Sunday schools if they are only enlisted, trained, and definitely set to the task of teaching.

Another imaginary obstacle in the way of grading a Sunday school is the prevalent idea that there is not enough room. Churches which catch the spirit of the Master will go all out in sacrificial giving to provide room. They will find that as they provide space, grade the Sunday school, set up more classes and departments, they reach more people. As they reach more people they will enlist more givers and so make it possible to provide more space to reach more pople. In fact a church cannot afford not to provide space.

If crowded quarters must be occupied temporarily, grading will help the situation. Several small classes can meet more effectively in a given area than can a few larger classes. Certainly with crowded conditions it is more than ever important to give each teacher a closely graded class in which he can minister to individual needs. However, no church can hope to maintain an effective, growing Sunday school in crowded, inadequate quarters.

Sometimes it is claimed that grading will cause pupils to leave the school. How often is the question asked, Would you grade a class if it would cause the members to quit the Sunday school? This looks like a real difficulty, but it is not. It is purely imaginary, because they will not quit the Sunday school if the matter is handled in the right way and the school is properly graded. The truth is that failure to grade has kept hundreds of pupils out of our schools in the past.

There will not be any trouble at this point if the pastor and superintendent will lead in a program of educating the people for grading. If the teachers are led to co-operate and use their influence with their pupils, they can get them to accept the grading plan. The trouble usually is not with the pupils but with the teachers.

IV. Removing the Difficulties in the Way of Grading

As has been suggested, all the difficulties and objections to grading the Sunday school ought to be gotten out of the way before the Sunday school is graded. This can be done if intelligence, wisdom, and patience are exercised by the pastor and superintendent.

1. *The Pastor and Superintendent Should Inform Themselves*

The pastor and the superintendent should have frequent conferences about the matter of grading the school, until they are in perfect accord. In addition to reading books and literature on the subject it would be helpful for them to visit a good graded Sunday school near by and study its methods and work.

2. *The Superintendent Should Hold a Conference of All the Teachers and Officers*

The superintendent should call all the teachers and officers together to confer about grading the school. The direction of the Holy Spirit should be earnestly sought. The benefits of grading should be intelligently presented by the superintendent and the pastor. The whole matter should be gone over and discussed in the most brotherly way, allowing everyone an opportunity to express his opinion. It will be easy to show that by grading the Sunday school its membership can be doubled within a few months and that the work of the teachers can be made more effective in every way. Likewise, it will be easy to show that a great Sunday school from every standpoint can be built up only after it is graded.

Often more than one conference will be necessary. After the teachers and officers have, through prayer and study, been convinced that it is for the best interest of all concerned to grade the school, all objections will disappear and harmony will prevail. Again, it should be said that a Sunday school should not be graded until there is assurance of co-operation on the part of the teachers and officers. A great deal of praying will often be necessary.

3. *The Teachers Should Be Enlisted and Adjusted*

The superintendent and the pastor should make from the church roll a list of the men and women in the membership of the church who apparently possess the qualifications of teachers. These commissioned leaders should then seek out such members and urge upon them the great need for teachers and the rare privilege which this call for service represents. The same sense of unworthiness which prompts an immediate refusal is excellent evidence of fitness to serve. The consecrated Christian will not long resist the appeal of his brethren to give himself to service which, in their judgment, he is qualified to render.

4. *A Season of Definite Training Should Be Held*

Let it be said again that there is enough good teaching material in every church to take care of the Sunday school situation if this material is developed. Often many of the best men and women refuse to undertake the great task of teaching in the Sunday school because they feel their incompetency and lack of training.

Just at this point the Sunday School Training Course can give help. Let the pastor and superintendent organize a training class for a week or two weeks of intensive study, teaching BUILDING A STANDARD SUNDAY SCHOOL and perhaps one of the other books of the Sunday School Training Course to these newly qualified officers and teachers as well as to all who have been teaching.

This will give them a good start in their work and an insight into their duties that they could not get in any other way. Confidence in themselves will readily be gained as they get a knowledge of how to do the work presented in this study. Classes should be conducted at intervals all through the year for the study of other books in the training course. In addition, a functioning weekly officers and teachers' meeting will furnish effective in-service training for Sunday school workers.

V. The Actual Work of Grading

To grade the Sunday school properly it is necessary to do it all at one time. Some suggest that the best way is to do it gradually. Not so. A Sunday school will not grow into a graded condition; things do not naturally become orderly or systematic. The tendency is in the other direction.

Every department in a Sunday school is related to every other department; every class is related to every other class and every individual pupil is related to every other pupil. One may think that he has one part of the school graded while the other parts are ungraded, and that sooner or later the entire school will become graded. Not so. It is almost impossible to maintain a graded class or a graded department unless the whole school is graded, because of the relations existing between departments, classes, and pupils. In maintaining a graded Sunday school, promotions are necessary, and there can be no such thing unless the whole school is graded.

1. *Preparing for Grading Day*

Although a school may be graded at any time during the year, the easiest time to do it is on the last Sunday in September, since the new Sunday school year starts in October. When the grading is done at some other time in the year, it is based on the pupil's classification age on the preceding October first. This is his age on the nearest birthday at that time. In other words, April 1 is used as the dividing point in classifying the pupil in October, and this is his classification age until the next October.

It is best to secure the needed information prior to grading day, work out the grading on paper, and enlist the needed teachers and officers. This will save confusion and errors on grading day.

If the school is being graded for the first time, or if the Six Point Record System is being installed, the first step is to secure a Classification Slip, Form 10, filled out for each member of the Sunday school. Any slips which have not been secured in advance through visits in the homes must be filled in on grading day. Slips for the little children will be filled in by their parents or others who bring the children. Older pupils will fill in their own slips, but all information given by Primaries, Juniors, and even Intermediates should be verified in visits to the homes.

Immediately following grading day every absentee should be visited, his classification slip secured, and a check made to see that his name is on the proper class roll. Whenever a new roll is made for any age group, every name from the former Sunday school roll must appear on roll somewhere. No name is dropped nor left off new rolls unless the pupil has died, moved away, or joined another Sunday school.

2. *Grading the Pupils*

If the school has been ungraded or operating on a class basis, it may be necessary to have all ages assemble together for the initial step of grading. Grade the pupils first into the age groups as listed in the Standard. When each group has moved to its own space, grade further within the group, as needed.

If departments are already in existence, each would meet in its own room and the grading proceed from there, as indicated. The total possibilities for each age group, not the present enrolment, should determine how closely each needs to be graded, and what organization is set up.

The Nursery children (ages birth through three): The workers should take these children to their assigned rooms. The help of parents may be needed in the Nurseries to secure the necessary information and to help the children get adjusted. If possible, separate rooms should be provided for the infants, creepers, toddlers, two-year-olds, and three-year-olds. At the very least, the bed-babies should be separated from the others.

The Beginners (ages 4-5): The Beginner workers and children should be assigned a place where they can always be to themselves for the entire session of the Sunday school, and function as a department, even if there are only five or six children. In larger schools there should be a department for about every thirty possibilities, with the age range limited to one year.

The Primaries (ages 6, 7, and 8): If space can be provided for Primaries to meet to themselves for all the Sunday school session, set them up as a department, even if only six or eight children are enrolled. When possible, grade on a close age basis into three or more departments with from twenty to thirty-five possibilities assigned to each.

The Juniors (ages 9-12): Even the smallest school should provide at least one class for Junior girls and one for Junior boys. If possible these two classes should form a department. When a department for ages nine through twelve enrols sixty to seventy-five, two departments of a two-year age range are needed. In many schools there should be four Junior departments, one for each year. When a department has from fifty to sixty enrolled in a single year and other prospects are available, an additional department should be provided. There should be a class for every six to ten possibilities.

The Intermediates (ages 13-16): Intermediate grading should parallel that for Juniors, with as many classes for Intermediates as for Juniors.

The Young People (ages 17-24): Every school should provide at least one class for men and one for women in this age range. If possible these two classes should form a department. There should also be a separate class for married young women, ages seventeen through twenty-four, and a similar class for the married men in this age range. In larger schools the trend is toward multiple departments, with separate provision for married Young People, and single Young People. Many schools provide a department for each year, at least for the seventeen-, eighteen-, and nineteen-year-olds. In college communities separate departments should be maintained for the nonresident Young People. There should be a class for every eight to fifteen possibilities in the younger Young People's departments, and for every eight to twenty possibilities for the older Young People.

Young People in the armed services should be reached by the Military Service Membership Plan. (Information may be secured from the Sunday School Department, Baptist Sunday School Board, Nashville 3, Tennessee.)

The Adults (ages 25 and up): If proper preparation has been made, Adults will gladly accept close age grading and annual promotion. An Adult department may be set up with two classes, one for men and one for women. However, few churches could not have at least four classes for Adults—two for men and two for women. More effective teaching can be done when there are classes graded to a narrow age range. There should be a class for every ten to forty Adult possibilities. Progressive churches are moving toward multiple departments for Adults, with the age range in each department limited to ten years, five years, or even less.

Great care must be exercised when Adults, or other age groups, are graded to make sure that every person who has been enrolled is reclassified and placed in his proper age group. Persistent visitation of chronic absentees may be needed to get their classification slips filled out, so that they can be assigned to the proper classes. No name should be dropped or lost from the roll because of grading. A name is not removed unless an individual has moved away, died, or joined another Sunday school.

VI. KEEPING THE SCHOOL GRADED

The Sunday school, although graded as previously suggested, if left to itself will soon get back to an ungraded state. However, it is easy to keep it graded if the proper methods are employed.

1. *Install the Six Point Record System*

The Six Point Record System, where correctly installed and operated, will aid greatly in keeping the school graded. In fact, the working of this system will practically, of itself, keep the Sunday school graded. Classifying pupils according to information on the classification slip is the first step in introducing this system. Added information and samples of the Six Point Record System will be sent free on application to the Baptist Sunday School Board, Nashville, Tennessee.

2. *Elect a Classification Officer*

An officer should be appointed in every Sunday school to look after the classification. In small schools this officer would be known as classification superintendent. He might also be the associate superintendent, one of his duties being to see that the school is kept properly graded. In large schools the general secretary is the proper classification officer, assisted by the department associate superintendents and secretaries, who classify all pupils as they enter their own departments. In every school there should be one person definitely charged with keeping the school graded.

3. *Observe Annual Promotion Day*

A Sunday school may be properly graded and kept graded for a year, but at the close of the year it will be ungraded unless there is a promotion day, at which time pupils are promoted from class to class and from department to department. The last Sunday in September is generally observed as annual Promotion Day in the Sunday schools in this country. It can be made a most delightful occasion.

Pastors, superintendents, if your school is not graded, take up the question at once, study it thoroughly, consult your officers and teachers and all together agree to grade your Sunday school, and then grade it.

QUESTIONS FOR REVIEW

1. Discuss the importance of the Sunday school being graded.

2. What is the basis for grading the Sunday school? What is the main purpose in all Sunday school work?

3. Mention and discuss three reasons for grading the Sunday school.

4. State the real difficulties in the way of grading the Sunday school.

5. How keep the Sunday school graded?

BAPTIST LITERATURE

Standard requirement:

Southern Baptist Sunday school literature prepared for the teachers and pupils in the various age groups shall be used throughout the school.

There are two general systems of Bible lessons offered by the Sunday School Board of the Southern Baptist Convention. They are known as the Uniform Lesson Series and the Graded Lesson Series.

The foregoing requirement is stated simply and means exactly what it says. Certainly Baptist Sunday schools should use Baptist literature.

I. REASONS WHY BAPTIST SUNDAY SCHOOLS SHOULD USE BAPTIST LITERATURE

Many reasons could be given as to why Baptist Sunday schools should use Baptist literature. This limited discussion will deal briefly with only three.

1. *Because of Its Doctrinal Integrity*

Baptist Sunday school pupils should have the Baptist interpretation of the Scriptures. The Bible interpretations in our Sunday School Board's literature can nowhere be excelled in regard to scriptural accuracy and doctrinal correctness. Three outstanding facts make this true. First, the editors and lesson writers of the Sunday School Board are staunch Baptists, as well as men and women of unquestioned scholarship. Second, minute care is constantly taken in the preparation of these lessons. Several careful Bible students read every sentence for the purpose of testing its rightness. Third, all our lesson treatments and periodicals are subjected to the closest scrutiny by individuals and groups both within and without our fellowship.

These are safeguards which insure the doctrinal integrity of the treatments in the Board's periodicals. Like safeguards are not thrown around the lessons prepared by individuals and other groups.

2. *Because of Its Intrinsic Value*

In every particular the periodicals of the Southern Baptist Sunday School Board are able to stand on their own merits in any comparison. In price they run lower than the average of other publishers' periodicals of like class. In attractiveness of style, design, decoration, and material they rank with the very best modern production of high-grade magazines. In content they include a range of material and illustrations that draws upon all known sources, far and near, offering a comprehensive volume of high-grade treatment. So, while meeting the obligations of economy, these lesson periodicals also offer the best possible literary content and attractive form, in addition to their spiritual message.

3. *Because of Service Rendered by the Board*

The Sunday School Board is an agency of the Southern Baptist Convention. This great institution belongs to Southern Baptists and a comprehensive grasp of its large and varied ministries should make them proud of it. It is a mistake to think of it as just a publishing house—a great business concern. It is all this and vastly more— it is a vast missionary agency. There is scarcely any phase of Southern Baptist work anywhere which has not received material aid out of the earnings of the Sunday School Board. The Board's margin of profit on each periodical and separate item is so small that even a minimum reduction in the price would wipe it out, yet its volume of business is so large that many thousands of dollars are earned each year, practically all of which go into the promotion of different phases of the work of Southern Baptists.

Every time a Sunday school orders literature from the Sunday School Board and pays its bill it may have the satisfaction of knowing, not only that it has secured the best of materials at the lowest price, but that it is also co-operating with some thirty thousand other Baptist churches and Sunday schools in enabling the Sunday School Board to promote and foster the most effective and extensive teaching and training program of any denomination of Christians in the world. This phase of the work of the Board is carried on in co-operation with each of the state mission boards of the various states comprising the Southern Baptist Convention.

Also, the Sunday School Board each year makes worthy contributions to the promotional budget of the Southern Baptist Convention, the work of the Woman's Missionary Union, the various Southern Baptist theological seminaries, the Carver School of Missions and Social Service (formerly W.M.U. Training School), and many other phases of denominational work. In addition the Board bears the expense of printing and distributing thousands of free denominational tracts that cover a wide range of subjects, and gives away thousands of Bibles, books, and periodicals in promoting the work. When all of these things are considered, it will be seen that the Board is vitally related to Southern Baptist work in so many ways that its earnings are practically necessary for the maintenance of these things.

This great missionary service rendered by the Board then becomes an added reason for the local support of every missionary Baptist who considers himself a part of the Southern Baptist Convention. In view of such support, the Board always welcomes suggestions concerning any phase of its work.

II. THE PLACE OF LESSON LITERATURE IN BIBLE STUDY

As the great main purpose of the Sunday school is to teach the Bible, let us carefully consider the place and power of the lesson literature in the Sunday school plan of Bible study.

1. *A Plan of Bible Study*

Whenever the Bible is adequately or intelligently studied, there must be a definite, comprehensive plan—a guide for the work. This is true whether the study occurs in a Christian college, a theological seminary, or in an individual church or Sunday school—whether the study is undertaken by an individual or by groups.

The Bible is a gigantic storehouse of all kinds of riches. Within its vastness there is the solution for every problem, the balm for every wound, and the answer to every need the world has ever known. This great truth is the very reason why there must be a plan for its study—a guide for the glorious undertaking of entering its portals with the determined will to perceive and appropriate its message.

Such then is the place of lesson literature in the Sunday school plan for Bible study. The literature carries a well-conceived, definite, comprehensive, and continuous plan for the study of the Bible.

A party of friends spent a most delightful two hours in following a guide through one of the interesting caverns in the beautiful Shenandoah Valley of Virginia.

Under the skilful direction of the practiced guide and with his enthusiastic explanations there were revealed many glorious marvels of beauty and natural wonder. Of course, with flashlights, ropes, and an unusual spirit of intrepid daring, they might have negotiated the trip without the guide, but even so, it is likely that much of its wonder would have been lost or misunderstood or not appreciated.

So it is that the Sunday school lesson literature, produced with prayerful dependence on the Holy Spirit, provides and becomes a guide for Bible study.

2. *A System of Bible Study Helps*

Surely everyone—preacher, teacher, and pupil—stands in need of all possible reliable help in the stupendous matter of studying the Holy Scriptures. Surely no worthy person would claim that the capacities of any human mind are, or could be, sufficient to compass the whole field of Bible revelation. But the Holy Spirit uses human minds to make his truths clear.

The Lord Jesus, as a boy, sought the help of lesson discussion with the doctors in the Temple. The apostle Paul learned the ancient Hebrew Scriptures both in his home and through an extended school career, and after his conversion sought out Peter and, no doubt, others to secure helps on the life and works of Jesus. Luke clearly states in the dedication which begins his Gospel that he has before him written accounts of the life of Jesus, which he proposes to use as "helps" in the preparation of his account. Not that any of these were wholly controlled or dominated by what they found in every source, but using these things and praying for the Holy Spirit's guidance, they pressed on to a fuller comprehension of the divine will of God, revealed through sacred writings and through consecrated lives. This then should be the constant attitude of Sunday school leaders and teachers.

It is the office of the Sunday school lesson literature to provide the best possible system of helps, prepared in full dependence on the Holy Spirit, by the best scholars and writers available to assist teachers and students in the constant and effective study of the world's greatest Book—the Source Book of all worthwhile life.

3. *A Vehicle for Applying Bible Study to Life*

It has been suggested that the Bible is a living book on life—to be applied to life today. This should be a constant emphasis. Our Bible is not just the sacred literature of a broken and despised people; it is the living Word of God for every human being alive today. It has in it the medicine for every sickness, the payment for every debt, the answer to every heart-searching query, and the way of life for every lost soul who is willing to follow its teaching to the foot of Calvary's cross.

As the Book on life it is not to be studied merely in the atmosphere of history, even spiritual history; but it is to be studied as the present-day guidebook for the life of every individual who can be brought under its influence.

The lesson literature, then, with its plans and helps for Bible study, aims always at the study and teaching of the Bible in such a way as to make it applicable and practical in the life of every pupil.

The place, then, of the lesson literature in a Sunday school is to offer a definite, adequate plan for Bible study best adapted to the different age groups and to provide a system of Bible study helps that will be of wide and effective use in understanding the Word of

God and in projecting its teachings into the hearts and lives of all who can be brought under its influence.

III. The Uniform Series

The Uniform Series for Sunday schools is the oldest and most widely used of the lesson systems. It had its beginning about 1872 and has since continued to grow in reach and to improve in quality.

1. *The Plan of the Uniform Series*

We have already insisted in this chapter that an outstanding necessity in a Sunday school's work of projecting Bible study is for a plan and a system of helps. From some sources has come the criticism that the courses of the Uniform Series were entirely too scattered and incomplete and therefore inadequate. Of course there is much that can be and is to be desired in Bible study beyond the plans and provisions contained in the Uniform Series. However, this series provides a balanced, progressive, comprehensive, and delightful plan that challenges our whole Sunday school constituency of pastors, officers, teachers, and pupils and offers full scope for any amount of intensive Bible research. Let us consider these lessons briefly.

(1) *Bible lesson courses.*—The content of the Uniform Series is avowedly Bible centered. These lesson courses are built in cycles of six years.

Bible selections are carefully made, and short courses of different types are introduced. These are chronological courses, topical courses, character study courses, and the like. Outlines are available.

Concerning these lessons, Dr. Howard P. Colson, editor in chief of Sunday school lesson courses for the Baptist Sunday School Board, has said: "Over a period of years the Uniform Lessons give a remarkably well-balanced program of Bible study. The life of Christ is kept central. There are also units on great Bible characters and Bible history. Each of the various types of writing found in the Word of God are included. Other units make a topical approach, using such themes as great doctrines of the Bible, growth in Christian living, the moral teachings of the Bible, etc. By keeping us anchored in God's Word, these lessons are a marvelous means of winning pupils to a saving faith in Jesus Christ and of developing them in Christian living and service."

As will be shown, the general topic and Scripture selections are made by a committee on Uniform Lessons. They prepare lesson adaptations for all age groups, from the Primary up. Our Southern Baptist Sunday School Board works out its own adaptation for the younger age groups. The same general lesson passage as for the Intermediates, Young People, and Adults is used, but the lessons are adapted for the different groups through the choosing of subjects, memory verses, and material suitable for use in teaching these younger ages. This service has been and is most significant and helpful. These adaptations are also widely used by other denominations.

(2) *The lesson makers and how the lessons are made.*— The Uniform Lessons are generally and widely used by many denominations, but not in the same form and treatment. Our arrangement and treatment of these lessons come to us in the following manner:

The Committee on the Uniform Lessons is made up of a membership of about sixty-nine representatives of the different co-operating denominations. Southern Baptists are represented on this Committee by several of our best Bible scholars and denominational leaders.

This Committee meets and agrees upon the Uniform Series prospectus. They build the course in its cycles, selecting the Bible material to be used and the different short course themes and subjects. Also they select for each Sunday's lesson a Scripture passage, a memory passage, a devotional reading, and department topics. This material is selected and published some two or three years in advance.

The lesson prospectus prepared by the Committee on Uniform Lessons is then taken by the editorial forces of our Baptist Sunday School Board. Careful examination is made of every subject and text, such changes being made as are deemed advisable.

After the lesson selections and adaptations are all agreed upon and approved, wide search is made for the very best Southern Baptist writers that can be found. They are enlisted to prepare the lesson material. When this material is received in the editorial offices, it is subjected to careful reading and constructive criticism. In the accomplishment of this monumental editorial task every effort is made to do the work that will result in providing our constituency with the very wisest and best treatment of each Bible lesson.

2. *The Uniform Lesson Literature*

The various periodicals that carry the Uniform Lesson treatments are described briefly on the next several pages.

(Although they are not based on the Uniform Lesson Scripture passages, the Nursery and Beginner materials are included here because they are group graded material meant for use in all Sunday schools. For a fuller description see pp. 80-81.)

Sunday with Two-Year-Olds is a worker's quarterly.

Letters for Parents of Two-Year-Olds are to be distributed to parents and used in visitation.

Pictures for Two-Year-Olds are large teaching pictures.

Sunday with Three-Year-Olds is a teacher's book.

Now I Am Three is a home book for children and parents.

Pictures for Three-Year-Olds are large teaching pictures.

Beginner Bible Story is a set of leaflets for each child and his parents.

Beginner Teacher is a quarterly for all Beginner workers.

Beginner Teaching Pictures are large pictures.

Sunday School Primary Pupil is the periodical carrying the lesson material for children from six through eight years of age. Two pages of beautiful pictures lithographed in four colors illustrate the lessons. These colored pictures include both Bible and present-day subjects. There are also frequent illustrations in black and white. Carefully selected memory work is included as well as a special memory verse for each lesson. Additional stories and workbook pages provide interesting activities for the children and materials which may enrich the teaching on Sunday.

Primary Teacher, a quarterly, is planned for teachers of the classes which use the *Sunday School Primary Pupil*. It provides three pages of lesson directions for each Sunday. These include not only an exposition of the Bible text, but also suggestions as to how the lesson may be taught. In addition, the magazine section carries program suggestions, seasonal materials, child study articles, and stories.

Primary Uniform Lesson Pictures are for class and department use. There are twelve pictures lithographed in four colors on durable cardboard. New pictures are issued each quarter.

Sunday School Junior Pupil is a quarterly planned for boys and girls from nine to twelve years of age inclusive.

Included in each lesson are workbook devices, questions, and explanatory notes on the Bible text. Special memory work is suggested for each lesson, in addition to the usual memory verse. Two pages of Bible and present-day pictures in four colors are to be cut out and matched to the lessons.

The *Junior Teacher* is a quarterly publication with illustrated cover and is planned especially to meet the needs of teachers of boys and girls from nine through twelve years of age. Each weekly treatment gives study helps and a suggested program, including songs, memory work, stories, etc. There is also a magazine section which carries much practical help for all who teach Juniors.

Junior Uniform Lesson Pictures are prepared for Junior classes and departments using Uniform Lessons. Each quarter there are twelve new pictures lithographed on durable cardboard.

The *Sunday School Intermediate Pupil* is for boys and girls thirteen through sixteen years of age. This quarterly carries the Intermediate topic, lesson text, "Golden Text," daily Bible readings, and a treatment of the lesson text adapted to the Intermediate pupils.

The *Intermediate Teacher* is a quarterly publication for the teachers and leaders of Intermediate pupils who use the Uniform Lesson quarterly. For each lesson there is given an exposition of the Bible material, an analysis of pupil experiences and needs as they are related to the lesson truth, and a suggested teaching procedure. There is a supplementary magazine section carrying helpful material on the subject matter of the lessons, adolescent characteristics and problems, and teaching techniques and plans.

Sunday School Young People, issued each quarter, contains a treatment of each lesson written expressly for Young People from seventeen through twenty-four. Introduction, outline, and explanation culminate in a message to Young People, followed by questions or suggestions designed to stimulate creative thinking and courageous application.

Sunday School Adults is a quarterly publication prepared for mature men and women. It carries the lesson text, Golden Text, daily Bible readings. It has a most comprehensive treatment of the lesson and makes a strong appeal to men and women who desire to do some real Bible study. Suggestions are given to provoke helpful discussion of Adult problems as they are related to the lesson.

On the Wing with the Word is a vest-pocket quarterly adapted from *Points for Emphasis,* our pocket commentary on the International Sunday school lessons, first published in 1918, and appearing annually since.

The Teacher is a monthly magazine for teachers of Young People or Adults, with a special explanation of the lesson, and sections showing how to prepare and how to present the lesson to the men and women in these age ranges, using various teaching methods. It also contains each month special articles on Bible study and teaching. Every general and department officer and teacher in these advanced grades should be provided, by the school, with a copy of *The Teacher* each month.

The Sunday School Builder is a magazine dealing with every phase of Sunday school organization and administration. It should be furnished to every teacher and officer in the school and made available to the officers of Adult and Young People's classes. The editorials by staff writers and contributions from front-line workers afield emphasize actual achievement rather than untried theory. The write-ups and articles are illustrated with photographs, pictures, and drawings. There are articles, program helps, and other material for workers with each age group.

3. *Practical Values of the Uniform Lesson Series*

This great series of Sunday school Bible lessons has wrought marvelously in the history of the Sunday school movement. It has been constantly improved and the best possible study is being given to it by many of the world's greatest Bible scholars and Sunday school workers. This series will continue to serve greatly in its field and is altogether worthy of its place. Following are given suggestively some of the practical values of this series:

(1) *Adequate and practical.*—Woodrow Wilson said, "The Sunday school is the world's greatest school for the teaching of the world's greatest Book." The lesson series used to produce this conviction in the heart and mind of this president was the Uniform Lesson system. When consideration is given to our Southern Baptist Sunday school membership possibilities of around fifteen million, and when the conditions of enlistment are studied, it will be found that the broad general approach to Bible study as contained in the Uniform Series is both a practical and an adequate course with which to go about this gigantic task.

(2) *Especially fits the smaller schools.*—The vast majority of our Southern Baptist Sunday schools average less than 200 in enrolment. Thousands of schools have enrolments under one hundred each. For these schools the Uniform Lessons are the best available, and present their leaders with Bible lesson plans and helps that are most practical and productive.

(3) *Challenges all Young People and Adults to Bible study.*—The Uniform Lessons are almost universally used for Young People and Adults. Perhaps many times they

are really more abused than used. However, they constitute a great outstanding and attractive challenge to this largest group of Sunday school pupils.

(4) *Economical.*—Comparisons will show that the Uniform Lesson literature produced by our Sunday School Board is most economical, when one considers the quality and quantity of content that it has. It is prepared and sold to the churches at very little above actual cost. In fact the margin is so small that if it were sold at actual cost each individual church would notice little reduction in its literature bill. That the Sunday School Board is able to have money out of this sale to do denominational promotional work is possible merely because of the tremendous volume of sales.

(5) *Simplifies assembly programs in class schools.*— Perhaps the part of the average Sunday school session that needs help as much as, or more than, any other part is the assembly program, whether it is the opening or closing part of the Sunday school period. One secret of having a successful assembly program is to correlate it with the lesson for the day. The Uniform Series, with the different age group adaptations, makes possible correlated assembly programs in schools which cannot provide a separate assembly for each age group.

(6) *Effective lesson study at the weekly officers and teachers' meeting.*—Reference to the chapter in this book on the weekly officers and teachers' meeting will reveal that the success of such a meeting depends upon getting the right plan. There are right plans for the conduct of this meeting where either type of lessons is used, but without doubt it is easier to handle a teaching improvement period in the small school where several age groups are represented, if they are all using adaptations of the same basic course.

(7) *Aids in getting family home study.*—In families where there are several children and where daily worship is observed, there is the fine opportunity of using the daily Bible readings and references, centering the Bible study of the family during these daily periods around the Sunday school lesson which all of them need to be preparing for the following Sunday morning. The task of getting the Bible studied in the homes by the pupils is made easier when the family follows the daily Bible readings which are carried in *Home Life,* A Christian Family Magazine recommended for distribution to every family represented in the Sunday school.

IV. THE CLOSELY GRADED LESSON SERIES

With the advent of the closely graded Sunday school and its teaching units for each age from the Nursery through the Intermediate department, there came the opportunity and the consequent demand for a closely graded lesson literature, with all the pedagogical advantages which could thus be obtained. In the closely Graded Lessons, Southern Baptist Convention Series, there is afforded opportunity not only for teaching the great fundamental truths of our common Christianity, but also for the indoctrination of our own people in the great truths which we hold and which we believe to be essential to New Testament Christianity.

1. *The Aim of the Closely Graded Lessons*

The Graded Lessons share with the Uniform the three-fold general aim of all Christian education, namely:

To lead the unconverted pupils toward God—teaching them about God and about Jesus, God's Son

To win unconverted pupils to Christ, bringing them into personal relationship with Jesus as their Saviour from sin, with resulting oneness in purpose and spirit with God

To help converted pupils develop an increasingly Christlike spirit, leading them to study and strive to become more and more like Jesus in attitude and in conduct

The Graded Lessons make it their specific purpose to take advantage of the closely graded set-up, and give the pupils those lessons from the Word of God which will best meet their needs at each stage of their development.

Some practical results of this guiding principle are as follows:

First, each lesson is definitely chosen with the physical, mental, and spiritual needs of growing, developing pupils in mind. Second, the lessons increase in difficulty, from year to year, in both material and method, thus making use of the pupils' growing powers and understanding. Third, with close grading the teacher teaches the same set of lessons each year to a class of the exact age for which the lessons are prepared. Thus he can acquire great skill in presenting the lessons to meet the individual needs of his pupils. Fourth, in the course of years the pupils have not only a complete study of those passages of God's Word best suited to their grasp and use, but they have again and again those passages most effective in bringing them into saving knowledge of Jesus and training them in his way of life.

2. *The Plan of the Closely Graded Lessons*

Outlines are made by capable committees under the leadership of the Graded Lesson editors of the Sunday School Board of the Southern Baptist Convention. After the outlines are completed and approved, there comes the same search for writers and the same painstaking editing and preparation for publication as was described in connection with the Uniform Series. In the completed plan the Graded Lesson Series offers a separate course of fifty-two lessons for each year; thus pupils of any one year will have different lessons from the pupils of the other years.

The lessons are so graded as to lead gradually from the themes of one year to those of the next year, thus giving systematic instruction in Bible teachings.

In order to install properly and use Graded Lessons to the best advantage, one must have a correct understanding of the plan and purposes of these lessons and of the methods of using them.

3. *The Closely Graded Lesson Literature*

Sunday with Two-Year-Olds is a quarterly which suggests procedures for workers with this age group on Sunday morning—both for the Sunday school hour and during the preaching service.

Letters for Parents of Two-Year-Olds are a set of thirteen letters issued quarterly to help parents teach religion to their children. They are distributed when parents call for their children and in visitation in the home.

Pictures for Two-Year-Olds are a set of eighteen beautiful colored large pictures carefully selected to aid in teaching this age group.

Sunday with Three-Year-Olds is a teacher's book issued quarterly, giving a suggested procedure and lesson material for each Sunday in working with three-year-olds.

Home Books for Three-Year-Olds, a series of four books, is issued quarterly to help parents provide Christian home teaching for three-year-olds.

Pictures for Three-Year-Olds, a series of eighteen pictures lithographed in four colors, are for use in the Nursery on Sunday. The same sets are used throughout the year.

Beginner Bible Story offers a set of thirteen beautiful, four-color leaflets for the child. Each leaflet provides a colored picture, a simple Bible story, and a Bible verse. Frequently there is a note for parents, a song, a poem, or other useful item. Fresh materials are provided each quarter.

The *Beginner Teacher* is a quarterly teacher's book, which is improved each year. In addition to practical lesson discussions for each Sunday, this publication offers general articles on new ideas and methods, with some child-life stories. Order a copy for each of your workers with Beginners. Printed new every quarter.

Beginner Teaching Pictures are a set of beautiful pictures, lithographed in four colors on durable cardboard. Definite suggestions for the use of each picture are included in the *Beginner Teacher.* There are twelve large pictures in each set. Fresh pictures are provided for every quarter.

Primary Teacher's Book, a manual for teachers, is published in four quarterly books for each of the three years, six, seven, and eight—twelve books in all. Each book gives suggested procedures and lesson material for each Sunday in the quarter.

These lessons feature the use of pictures designed to enrich the child's appreciation of the Bible truth and to motivate and encourage the practice of this truth in life situations. The pupils' books contain the best pictures available—many in full color—of both Bible and child-life situations. There are six teaching pictures in each teacher's book, all in full color. The use of these pictures and some of those in the pupils' books is provided for in the teaching procedure of the various lessons. Thus every teacher has available, without additional cost, pictures to enrich Bible teaching on the level of the child's interest.

Primary Pupils' Books, four copies for each year, are beautifully printed in full color, with the size of the type, the length of the lines, the layout of the pages especially adapted to the capacities of Primary children. Each book for each age group and each quarter carries a title which appeals to the interest of the pupil, as *Learning About God, Friends Near and Far,* or *Learning of God's Love.* The children have books just as attractive as their schoolbooks, books that stimulate personal pride, books to be a witness in the home, books for continual examination and study, books that seek to conserve in the hands of the children the message of the Bible about the problems of their varying experiences.

These books carry a workbook section for every lesson, which provides an interesting check on Bible knowledge and suggestions for activities during the weekdays. The experiences in these activities should mean spiritual growth.

Primary Picture Sets, in four sets of nine pictures each, are offered for use in Primary department assembly periods. They are to be used in connection with Primary Graded Lessons.

The *Primary Superintendent's Manual* provides a guidebook for superintendents, especially in the schools using the Graded Lessons. It is designed to set forth department activities, program materials, and lesson courses in order to make possible their most fruitful use.

Junior Teacher's Book is a teacher's textbook issued in four quarterly parts for each of the four years, nine through twelve, giving a suggested teaching procedure and lesson material for each Sunday in the year.

Junior Pupil's Book, a work and study book for pupils, is furnished in four quarterly parts for each year.

Junior Picture Sets, four sets of nine pictures each, are offered for enriching the department assembly periods. They are to be used in connection with Junior Graded Lessons.

Junior Superintendent's Manual, a handbook contains programs, program suggestions, and lesson outlines for the use of the superintendent of the Junior department.

The *Intermediate Teacher's Book,* is furnished in four quarterly parts, for each of the four years, thirteen through sixteen, giving a suggested procedure and lesson material for each Sunday in the year.

The *Intermediate Pupil's Book,* is a work and study book for pupils, furnished in four quarterly parts for each year.

The *Intermediate Superintendent's Manual,* is a guidebook for the department superintendent, with particular help on the Graded Lessons.

4. *Practical Values of the Graded Lessons*

Each lesson is chosen with reference to the pupil's needs and capacities, and is given in connection with experiences similar to those in which it is most likely to be needed. Hence it stands a good chance to carry over into the pupil's everyday life and be lived.

The methods suggested for teaching these lessons are in keeping with God's laws for growing minds and hearts. The lessons are presented in connection with the pupils' own experiences and as something they need to know; consequently the pupils are interested and want to learn.

The teaching suggestions provide for actually teaching the lessons, not telling or hearing, and make much provision for helping the pupils to learn by doing, or by personal experience, which is the most effective learning.

The teaching helps are so full and so complete that even the teacher who is without the advantages of a good biblical library and special training in pedagogy can use them with a feeling of confidence and power; the ideas and suggestions developed are so many and varied that each teacher can find something which appeals to his own interest and ability, and, at the same time, meets his pupils' needs.

The lessons are permanent, that is to say, the same lesson is to be used from year to year with the same age group, so the teacher not only may become thoroughly familar with his own lessons, but may get a general grasp of those the pupils have had before they came to him, and of those they are to have after they leave him. This long view makes for well-wrought continuity in the pupils' learning.

These closely Graded Lessons are offered especially for Sunday schools having at least a class for each age. Certainly every Sunday school having enrolled as many as five pupils of each age from four through eight years, or five pupils of each age and sex from nine through sixteen years, should have them divided into separate classes for each year. For such schools, and for all those with larger enrolments, the closely Graded Lessons are especially prepared.

V. Special Publications

In addition to the literature carrying the lesson materials, the Board publishes several special periodicals. Each of these is designed to have a part in carrying out the commission which the Lord Jesus Christ has given to his church.

1. *Home Life*, A Christian Family Magazine.

This monthly provides interesting material on building Christian home life. It is designed especially to stimulate and to help earnest Christian parents who are anxious to make their homes all that they should be.

Distribution of *Home Life* is through the Sunday school organization, each department being responsible for placing the magazine in the homes of its enrolment. It is used by the Cradle Roll and Extension departments as their official periodical.

2. *Illustrated Story Papers*

The story papers are planned to be used as an integral part of the spiritual training program of a Sunday school. They are carefully graded and carry stories and features which offer very practical help in teaching the pupils about the Christian life and leading them to strive toward these things.

Storytime fills a long-felt need for character building stories that present situations and problems which the child meets in everyday life. The poems and illustrations are within the experience of childhood. Children who have learned to read will enjoy the large, clear type, and the surprise stories of daily life. This is a four-page, illustrated, weekly story paper for children of the Beginner and Primary ages. In each issue there are stories and poems which show how the truths being taught in Sunday school and Training Union relate to the child's experience. Those who work with children will be assisted in the educational process by these stories, as they emphasize the objectives of the lesson taught, and unconsciously suggest right conduct. Mothers will like to read to the younger children these stories and poems.

The Sentinel is our four-page illustrated story paper for Juniors. The stories are full of action and present situations and problems which the boy and girl meet in everyday life. Bits of biography, portions of popular science, travel, sports, nature, and missionary articles enrich its pages. Appealing poetry, instructive articles, and attractive illustrations contribute toward making this paper an important part of the curriculum which we publish.

Upward is a sixteen-page illustrated weekly prepared for Intermediates. Its carefully balanced content of stirring stories of adventure and achievement, and absorbing articles on foreign lands, biography, science, sports, and travel will hold the reader's interest. The stories are illustrated by artists of proved ability, and well-chosen photographs enhance greatly the value of the articles. These factors combine with carefully selected editorials and verse to make a paper of definite interest and influence.

QUESTIONS FOR REVIEW

1. Give three reasons why Baptist Sunday schools should use Baptist literature.

2. What place has lesson literature in the study of the Bible in the Sunday school?

3. Give at least four values of the Uniform Bible Lessons.

4. Give the aim of the Graded Lessons.

5. Discuss the practical values of the Graded Lessons.

6

BIBLES

Standard requirement:

1. The Bible shall be used as the textbook of the school.

2. The officers and teachers shall provide opportunities for the pupils to use their Bibles in the school.

3. The officers and teachers shall encourage the pupils and their parents to engage in daily family Bible reading and prayer.

The Bible requirement of the Standard does not say that the Bible shall be brought but that it shall be used. Certainly every officer, teacher, and pupil should bring his Bible to the Sunday school, and this is provided for by a requirement of the Six Point Record System. These two requirements are not the same. The Six Point Record System is a pupil program and the Standard of Excellence is a school program. Nevertheless, the two requirements complement each other and are mutually helpful. The purpose of the Standard requirements is to encourage the use of Bibles by officers, teachers, and pupils. It would be of little value for pupils to bring their Bibles to the Sunday school and not use them. If all the pupils were to bring their Bibles to the Sunday school Sunday morning and no opportunity be given to use them, the requirement could not be met.

Bibles lying round in church buildings, in the pews and bookcases, unopened, would not meet this require-

ment. A Bible unused is a Bible lost. Just as the Bible
was lost in the house of God in the days of Josiah, so
may it be lost in our churches today. Not only are
Bibles lost in many of our Sunday schools and churches
but also in multitudes of homes. How often are Bibles
seen in bookshelves and on tables and are never used.

The writer spent a week once in a home which boasted
of owning more than a dozen different kinds of Bibles.
Everywhere one turned he would see Bibles; on tables,
in book cases, and on shelves; Bibles galore! Big Bibles,
little Bibles, fine Bibles, cheap Bibles—Bibles in five or
six different languages. But during the entire week not
one of these Bibles was used in any way so far as could
be seen—no family worship, no study of the Sunday
school lessons or Training Union topics. The Bibles in
that home were all lost.

I. THE PLACE OF THE BIBLE IN THE SUNDAY SCHOOL

The Bible should be used in the Sunday school by
pastor, superintendent, teachers, and pupils. It should
be given its rightful place and nothing should be allowed
to take its place or interfere with its use.

1. *The Bible, the Pupil's Textbook*

The Sunday school is a Bible school. The Bible is the
textbook, and the only textbook, used in the Sunday
school. And when the aims and purpose of the Sunday
school are considered no other textbook is needed. Good
lesson helps are of great value, and care should be taken
to provide the best helps possible, but they should not
be allowed in any measure to supplant the Bible. Certainly, as the textbook of the school, the Bible should be
brought and used.

Notice some things the Bible will do for those who
study it.

(1) *What the Bible will do for the lost*.—"From a child thou hast known the holy scriptures, which are able to make thee wise unto salvation through faith which is in Christ Jesus" (2 Tim. 3:15). What the Bible did for young Timothy, it will do for the lost pupils in the Sunday schools if they are led to study it.

It is ours to bring the lost pupils in our Sunday schools in touch with the Bible and to inspire them to study it. God will see to it that his Word is honored in their salvation. "For the word of God is quick, and powerful, and sharper than any twoedged sword, piercing even to the dividing asunder of soul and spirit, and of the joints and marrow, and is a discerner of the thoughts and intents of the heart" (Heb. 4:12).

(2) *What the Bible will do for the saved*.—The Bible is the Christian's food and makes him strong if he studies it. The apostle Paul said to the Ephesian elders: "I commend you to God, and to the word of his grace, which is able to build you up" (Acts 20:32). There is no such thing as a virile, vigorous Christian apart from the study of God's Word. The Sunday school should be a place where there is real Bible study, both for the purpose of saving the lost and building up and making strong stalwart Christian characters of those who acknowledge Christ as Saviour.

The study of God's Word, the textbook of the Sunday school, is also a safeguard to the Christian. It is his weapon of defense, "Thy word have I hid in mine heart, that I might not sin against thee" (Psalm 119:11). It is also the Christian's weapon of offense, "And take . . . the sword of the Spirit, which is the word of God" (Eph. 6:17). The child of God needs to study the Bible. He needs to know it in order that he may be able to use it. We are talking about the place of the Bible in the Sunday school—what it will mean to the Christian who really studies it; how it will make him a strong, vigorous Christian; how it will make him a happy, singing Christian, keeping him from sin and in a state of mind and spirit where he can be of service at all times.

2. *The Bible, the Teacher's Tool*

It is said that "an instrument is just as skilful as the one who wields it, be it tongue or pen or sword or broom." This is largely true with the Bible. If the Sunday school teacher earnestly seeks the best for his pupils, he will bring it to them through the teaching of God's Word. The Bible is God's very Word. In Isaiah 55:10-11, God says, "For as the rain cometh down, and the snow from heaven, and returneth not thither, but watereth the earth, and maketh it bring forth and bud, that it may give seed to the sower, and bread to the eater: so shall my word be that goeth forth out of my mouth: it shall not return unto me void, but it shall accomplish that which I please, and it shall prosper in the thing whereto I sent it."

What a glorious task is that of the Sunday school teacher! What confidence and courage should these words bring to his heart! How they should challenge him to study and prepare himself to be a workman unashamed! God is far more concerned than the Sunday school teacher can ever be in saving the lost and in sanctifying the saved. He puts into the teacher's hands his Holy Word, the instrument with which to accomplish these blessed results, and stands ready to help and to see that the teacher who teaches his Word shall not fail.

II. How to Have the Bible Used in the Sunday School

Practically all are agreed that the things just discussed are true, yet in many of our Sunday schools there is too little of real Bible study or skilful Bible teaching. The practical side of this question needs discussion; therefore, let us study ways of having the Bible used in the Sunday school.

1. *The Superintendent's Part*

The superintendent is the responsible leader of the Sunday school and should function constantly in this matter of having the Bible used by teachers and pupils throughout the school.

(1) *Bring and use his own Bible.*—The superintendent, being the man in charge of the Sunday school, must lead in every good work. While he may not be the best Bible student in the Sunday school, yet he ought to be a real lover of the Bible, a real student of the textbook of the school over which he presides. His example will go far toward having the Bible studied and taught. Like Gideon, his motto should be, "Look on me, and do likewise." He should bring his Bible to the Sunday school every Sunday morning; he should show it and use it. It will be easy to get others to follow his example.

(2) *Include the Bible in his program.*—The Bible should be in evidence in the superintendent's program every Sunday, certainly before and often after the lesson study period. He should have readings of Scripture passages every Sunday morning. He should sometimes lead the reading himself, the school responding; sometimes two classes may read responsively; sometimes members may read passages related to the lesson. There are many ways of having the Bible used attractively at the beginning and close of the program. If the superintendent will plan for this, he will make it one of the most attractive features of his program.

(3) *Use the Six Point Record System.*—One of the most effective helps toward having Bibles used in the

Sunday school is by the use of the Six Point Record System. One of the requirements in this system is that the Bible shall be brought; and whenever due emphasis is placed on the record program, the pupils do bring their Bibles.

This bringing of his own Bible by the pupil becomes a constant demand upon the teacher to provide for its use. And while classroom Bibles, if actually used, will meet the requirement of the Standard, still it is easier and far better for each pupil to use his own Bible.

(4) *Train the teachers to use the Bible.*—The following discussion is concerned with the teacher's part in getting the Bible used in the Sunday school. However, it is the business of the superintendent to train the teachers in this important phase of their work. This may be done in connection with the regular weekly officers and teachers' meetings, monthly workers' conferences, during the special weeks of training, and in other ways.

2. *The Teacher's Part*

While the superintendent is the individual who is responsible, still the teacher is the one who should largely lead in the actual use of the Bible in the Sunday school on Sunday morning.

The teacher should bring and use his own Bible. From every standpoint the teacher who uses his Bible in teaching the lesson will have an advantage over the teacher who does not use his Bible in class, no matter how well he may know the lesson. He will certainly cover the lesson better. He will attract and hold the interest of his pupils better; he will inspire new confidence in the minds and hearts of his pupils by frequently reading short passages from the Bible. He will secure the interest of all his pupils by having some of them to read brief passages from the Bible. He will center the thoughts of his pupils on the lesson by using the Bible during the class period. He can settle all arguments by giving a "thus saith the Lord" and having the reference read from the Bible by some of his pupils. And, in the case of boys or girls, it will greatly help in maintaining order by having them search for passages, and read from the Book. This method will make a poor teacher a good teacher in a short while, and will make a good teacher a better one.

The teacher may assign references for pupils to look up at home. Often the best teaching the teacher will do, will be to assign certain incidents in the Bible for illustrating the next Sunday's lesson to be looked up and read by one or more pupils the following Sunday. Perhaps the teacher may get pupils to tell the story or incident in their own language. The Bible is a fruitful field of illustrations for every Sunday school lesson. The wise teacher will have his pupils laboring in this field day by day.

The teacher can, and certainly should, see that every pupil in the class has a Bible of his own and brings it to the Sunday school. It is simple and easy enough to find if each one of his pupils owns a Bible. The teacher can invoke the superintendent's co-operation where pupils are not able to buy Bibles. It is certainly easy to have a Bible fund in the church budget for purchasing Bibles for the pupils when wise to do so. "Love will find a way."

The foregoing applies to pupils from Junior age up. Primaries who have developed sufficient reading skill are encouraged to bring and use Bibles.

The Bible is God's Word. It is the Sunday school's only textbook. It will produce the peaceable fruits of righteousness in the lives of those who study it. It will bring courage and hope to discouraged hearts and lives.

By its use the Sunday school teacher can do mighty things for God. Let us see to it that our Sunday school officers, teachers, and pupils, all bring and use their Bibles.

QUESTIONS FOR REVIEW

1. Show how the Standard requirement and the Six Point Record System requirement on Bibles supplement each other.

2. How will the use of the Bible in the hands of the teacher insure success?

3. Who is chiefly responsible for having Bibles used in Sunday schools? Why?

4. Give four practical methods the superintendent may employ in securing the use of Bibles.

5. How does the Six Point Record System assist in having Bibles used?

7

PREACHING ATTENDANCE

Standard requirement:

1. An average of at least 70 per cent of the officers, teachers, and pupils above eight years of age attending the school shall remain for the preaching services.

2. The Beginners and Primaries shall be encouraged to remain for the preaching services.

The preaching attendance requirement is that 70 per cent of all those attending the Sunday school above eight years of age shall remain for the preaching service.

Some churches have children's meetings simultaneously with the morning preaching service and boys and girls who attend these other meetings are given credit for preaching attendance. This procedure not only does not meet this requirement literally, but it wholly misses the purpose and spirit of the requirement.

The purpose of this point is to put those who attend Sunday school into the morning preaching service, so that Bible study may be followed by a period of public worship. Any evasion of this requirement misses the point and is bad training for boys and girls, and men and women.

I. PUPILS NEED THE PREACHING SERVICE

Sunday school pupils need the opportunity the preaching service offers to worship God. They need the advantages it offers in an educational way. They need this habit formed in their lives because of its influence for good. They need the association of those who attend. They need the comforts of the gospel that come through the preached Word. They need the message of the gospel that is preached to the lost. They need both the social and the spiritual blessings it affords. They need the strong, wholesome meat of the gospel to counteract the weak, insipid, trashy food they get day by day from a thousand unreliable sources. All Sunday school pupils need the preaching service.

II. MANY SUNDAY SCHOOL PUPILS DO NOT ATTEND THE PREACHING SERVICE

It is a fact that large numbers of the members of city and town Sunday schools do not attend the preaching service Sunday morning.

Much complaint has been made, and many and grievous faults have been laid at the door of the Sunday school because of this. Many writers have put the blame for this condition entirely upon the Sunday schools, taking the position that, if it were not for the Sunday schools, the boys and girls and young people would attend the Sunday morning preaching service in great numbers. And some have even gone so far as to advocate doing away with the Sunday schools altogether in order to correct this deplorable condition. Would that remedy the evil? In other words, would abolishing the Sunday school increase the attendance at the preaching service? Most assuredly it would not. Do people who do not attend Sunday school regularly attend the preaching service in large numbers? All experience and observation teach us that they do not. A careful study of the causes for this condition will assist greatly in the solution of this perplexing problem.

III. SOME FALSE IMPRESSIONS

Before considering the real cause for so much lack of preaching attendance upon the part of Sunday school members, let us examine some false impressions concerning this important phase of our work.

1. *That the Services Are Too Long*

Many claim that the Sunday school and the preaching service combined are too long for boys and girls and young people to attend, and that they cannot stand the physical strain of coming to Sunday school at nine-thirty and remaining until the close of the preaching service at twelve o'clock.

Is it asking too much to expect boys and girls and young people to spend the entire forenoon of the Lord's Day in Bible study, worship, and praise? They need both the Sunday school and the service of worship and ought to have them. Furthermore, they should not get tired, as they are not compelled to occupy one position the entire time, since frequent opportunity is given for change of posture and for participation in the service.

Many of our strongest men and women, physically and certainly spiritually, have been regular attendants at both the Sunday school and preaching service since they were little children and cannot remember the time when they did not regularly attend both of these services. The contention made that it would injure the boys and girls physically to attend both the Sunday school and preaching services every Sunday morning is ridiculous and not substantiated by facts.

2. *That the Sermons Should Be Different*

It is claimed that sermons for boys and girls and young people should be essentially different from the average Sunday morning sermon, both in style and length.

As a result of this idea some pastors get the boys and girls together for a five- or ten-minute "sermonette." By some this is called the "Junior congregation," by others the "Junior church." It is a great mistake to think that boys and girls need, or even like, baby sermons or ragtime songs. They do not. They like good, solid, wholesome sermons. They like to sing the good gospel songs. They like to hear the Bible read and expounded. They can appreciate a good gospel sermon far better than many grownups and it is wrong to think they are not above ragtime songs and mushy baby sermons.

Even the little children can remember the pastor's text and can understand many things he says. A four-year-old child once heard a sermon from the text, "Sirs, we would see Jesus." During the sermon the preacher repeated the text many times and for many days and even weeks afterward the child at play around the home was frequently heard to repeat the text aloud to himself, "Sirs, we would see Jesus." This child was converted very early in life. Who knows but that very text was used of God for that purpose? Even though the children cannot comprehend many things in the sermon, they will receive everlasting impressions for good.

Statistics show that a vast number of children come into the Sunday school early in life, remain there for many years, and finally drop out of the Sunday school without finding Christ as Saviour. But statistics do not furnish information concerning children who have been in both the Sunday school and the preaching services regularly for any great length of time without being saved. It is believed to be practically impossible for a child to come into the Sunday school early in life and also be a regular attendant upon the preaching service without being saved by the time he reaches his early teens. God's promise is behind the preached word.

Therefore we should be mightily concerned about getting the Sunday school pupils to attend the preaching service Sunday morning. They need it. All need it. There is no need to worry about their health. They will survive the physical strain without damage to their precious bodies. The Holy Spirit can and will supply many deficiencies in the sermon, accompanying the message of the preacher to the hearts and consciences of the boys and girls, convicting them of sin and leading them to Christ, the sinner's only refuge.

3. *That Special Recognition Should Be Given*

Special recognition of their presence every Sunday is not at all necessary. That would not induce them to stay for the preaching service. They have just come from the Sunday school where they have been in prominence in the class or department. They are now in the service of worship, a totally different kind of service which, if they are in the habit of attending, they will soon learn to appreciate and love.

The presence of the young people and children in the preaching service Sunday after Sunday certainly would be an inspiration to any preacher and would influence him in the selection of texts, themes, and illustrations. And he would and should frequently speak of them and commend them for their faithful attendance. Yet that would not induce Sunday school pupils to attend in great numbers; and the omission of special recognition is not the reason for their nonattendance. We shall have to look deeper to locate the cause.

IV. THE REAL CAUSE

Sunday school pupils have not been trained to remain for the preaching service. Pastors, superintendents, and teachers are all guilty at this point. The Sunday school and the preaching service have been conducted as two distinct services, appealing to and meeting the needs of different classes of people. One is spoken as the Sunday school and the other as the "church service." The impression is made that one appeals to and meets the needs of children, boys and girls, and young people, and the other appeals to and meets the needs of mature men and women and is not adapted at all to the needs of children and young people.

Sunday school pupils have even been invited to go home by the dismissal of the Sunday school with a closing prayer in which the Lord is asked to "dismiss us now with thy blessings, go with us to our respective homes, and bring us back safely next Sunday morning."

V. SUNDAY SCHOOL PUPILS CAN BE INDUCED TO REMAIN

In order to secure regular attendance upon the preaching service on the part of the Sunday school pupils, it is necessary that intelligent, vigorous, and definite action be taken. Three ways will be suggested and discussed briefly, any of which will secure partial results in this direction. If all three are used, the results will be most gratifying and soon a large majority of Sunday school pupils will be found in attendance upon the services of worship every Sunday morning.

1. *Co-operation by the Officers and Teachers*

Let the superintendent of the Sunday school, backed up by the pastor, take up the matter in a conference with all the officers and teachers present. Let a perfect agreement be reached that all of the officers and teachers will co-operate by remaining for the preaching service and by urging their pupils to do so. The superintendent should make public announcement of this action from the platform Sunday morning and urge all members of the Sunday school to remain for the preaching service.

Where there are department officers, they should urge the same thing in their respective departments and all the teachers should exert every influence in persuading the pupils to remain. In this way a great many pupils will be induced to remain for the preaching service. They will soon get the habit and will greatly enjoy it.

A large majority of Sunday school pupils can be led to attend the services of worship as a result of this method. Still a more definite method should be added in order to secure a full attendance of the pupils.

2. *Installation and Correct Operation of the Six Point Record System*

There is absolutely no doubt of the effectiveness of the Six Point Record System in securing the attendance of Sunday school pupils at the preaching service. The system should be installed throughout the Sunday school according to the plans and suggestions set out in the book *The Six Point Record System and Its Use.*

The points above the Primary department should carry the following values:

Sunday School Attendance ....20 points
On Time ....10 points
Bible Brought ....10 points
Offering ....10 points
Prepared Lesson ....30 points
Preaching Attendance ....20 points
                                  ——
Total ....100 points

It will be noted that the same credits are given for Sunday school attendance as for preaching attendance. This will soon impress pupils with the idea that both of these services have equal claims upon their attention. However, it is a mistake to think that Sunday school pupils will attend the service of worship because they are given a credit of 20 points for doing so. Such an idea wholly misses the mark. It is not because a credit of 20 points is given pupils for attending the preaching service or the Sunday school that they attend either of these services. Neither will pupils bring their Bibles or an offering or prepare their lessons because they receive credit for doing so. The doing of any of these things cannot be secured by the use of artificial methods.

Then how does the Six Point Record System function in securing attendance at the preaching service? It is because the Sunday school has adopted the Six Point Record System and the school has agreed to co-operate in its use. Therefore, in order to secure attendance at the preaching service the superintendent should constantly urge every pupil to make a 100 per cent grade every Sunday.

It is the spirit back of the Six Point Record System that makes it vital and effective at any and all points. It should receive attention at each officers and teachers' meeting. Frequently on Sunday morning the teachers should explain to their pupils the meaning of the record system and the worth of each one of the six points in building character. They should urge every pupil to be a 100 per cent pupil.

The standing of classes and departments should be reported weekly. Likewise, the monthly grades of classes and departments should be reported. If possible these reports should be printed or mimeographed and distributed throughout the entire congregation. The grades of pupils up to and including the Intermediate department should be carefully made out and sent to their parents. The grades of pupils above the Intermediate department should be delivered to the pupils themselves.

In this way home co-operation may be secured. Parents not only will become interested in their children's being in the Sunday school on time, with a Bible and an offering, but they will also help the children in their lesson preparation and use their influence in having them remain for the preaching service.

No Sunday school intelligently using the Six Point Record System has yet reported failing to secure an attendance of at least 70 per cent of the Sunday school pupils upon the Sunday morning preaching service.

There is one other method which, if added to the two already discussed, will make it comparatively easy for any Sunday school to secure the attendance of a majority of its members at the regular service of worship Sunday morning.

3. *Use of the Unified or Combined Service*

The use of the Unified Service will be a great help at this point. This means combining the Sunday school session and the preaching service; that is, going from the Sunday school into the preaching service without intermission.

Will the boys and girls and young people remain for the preaching service? Certainly they will; and furthermore, they will soon learn to enjoy the service of worship and come to realize that it is as much for them as it is for fathers and mothers.

It is readily seen that in combining the Sunday school and the preaching service, detriment has not been done to either. Neither service has been abridged or infringed upon. On the contrary, both services have been greatly benefited.

Best of all, the Sunday school pupils—boys and girls and young people—will constitute an important part of the Sunday morning congregation. Their very presence should be an inspiration and help to the pastor. He will recognize in them his greatest opportunity to win souls. He will find himself studying for them, seeking for truths and lessons for them, searching for illustrations for them. Seeing them in his congregation regularly every Sunday morning, he will more and more get them and their salvation upon his heart; and lest there be loss, he will be constrained day by day to thrust in the sickle.

QUESTIONS FOR REVIEW

1. Should any other service be substituted for the preaching service?

2. Why should Sunday school pupils attend the preaching service?

3. What of the ability of Sunday school pupils to understand the pastor's sermon?

4. Discuss the real cause of Sunday school pupils not remaining for the preaching service Sunday morning.

5. What is the first thing that should be done in order to get them to remain?

6. Discuss how the use of the Six Point Record System will help.

7. Show how the unified or combined service contributes toward securing their attendance.

8

EVANGELISM

Standard requirement:

1. *The school shall be positively evangelistic.*

2. *The teachers shall earnestly seek to lead their pupils who are not Christians to a personal acceptance of Christ as Saviour and Lord.*

3. *The superintendent and pastor shall give frequent opportunities for the pupils who are not Christians to confess Christ publicly, and urge them to do so.*

The supreme business of Christianity is to win the lost to Christ. This is what churches are for. It was Christ's one supreme mission, according to his own words. "For the Son of man is come to seek and to save that which was lost" (Luke 19:19). "I am come that they might have life, and that they might have it more abundantly" (John 10:10). Surely then the Sunday school must relate itself to the winning of the lost to Christ as an ultimate objective.

Not only is this winning of the lost to Christ an all-important task, it is also a most attractive task. At summer assemblies, encampments, training schools, and Bible institutes, the class in evangelism is always large. Christian people love to study about it.

The soul-winning preachers and teachers are always attractive and never lack for hearers; and just as the throngs pressed upon Jesus when he was here, so today will people attend upon the ministry of the soul-winning preacher and the soul-winning teacher. Likewise, the soul-winning church will be a popular church and the soul-winning Sunday school will draw the multitudes into its membership.

There is no subject except prayer, perhaps, which commands the attention of Christian people so much as soul-winning. And yet it is practiced so little! Let us, therefore, consider anew the commanding and pressing importance of soul-winning in the Sunday school, and let us see how intensely real and practical it is.

I. THE SUNDAY SCHOOL IS THE CHURCH'S GREATEST SOUL-WINNING OPPORTUNITY

That the Sunday school is the most commanding opportunity of the churches today in the matter of soul-winning may be best understood by considering the following facts:

1. *Large Numbers of Lost People Are to Be Found in the Sunday School Membership*

The Sunday school is an outreaching agency; its business is to bring into its membership both those who are saved and those who are lost. A glance at any Sunday school roll, where any sort of organized effort is being made to build up the membership of the school, will disclose the fact that large numbers of the Sunday school members, especially among the young people and boys and girls, are not Christians.

In visiting churches one frequently hears the remark, "there are no lost people in this community," or "all the people in this community belong to some of the churches," or kindred expressions. If one will go carefully into the Sunday school situation anywhere, however, it will be found that this is a great mistake and that large numbers who are not Christians are to be found in every community.

Statistics gathered in the interest of the Sunday schools in the Convention over a period of years, show that, in Sunday schools which are constantly growing, more than three-fourths of the boys and girls nine to twelve years of age are not Christians; that more than half of those thirteen to sixteen years of age are not Christians; and that a little less than half of the Young People, seventeen through twenty-four, are not Christians. In schools which follow the methods which produce constant growth, lost people of all ages, including Adults, are constantly being enrolled and won to Christ. A growing Sunday school is the most effective factor known to insure perennial evangelism.

2. *The Taught People Belong to the Sunday School*

The use of the Bible makes the Sunday school a great evangelistic opportunity. In winning lost people to Christ the soul-winner has a great advantage if he is dealing with those who study the Bible. The approach is easy for the soul-winning teacher, for he has a real point of contact. His pupils are intelligent concerning the Scriptures. They also believe what the Bible says. The Holy Spirit works through the Word. A little Sunday school girl ten years of age made a public profession of her faith in Christ during a protracted meeting. To the question of the pastor as to when she had trusted Christ, she named a time, several weeks preceeding the meeting then in progress, during family worship as her father read the Scripture verse "The entrance of thy words giveth light" (Psalm 119:130).

3. *Those Who Are Most Susceptible to the Gospel Message Belong to the Sunday School*

The children, the boys and girls, and the young people, constitute a large part of the membership of all Sunday schools and they are most susceptible to the gospel message. Their presence makes the Sunday school a fruitful evangelistic opportunity. They are not yet sin hardened and habit bound. This is God's time for salvation, the best time, the easiest time! "Remember now thy Creator in the days of thy youth, while evil days come not, nor the years draw nigh" when the sweet and pure cease to charm and sinful habits fetter and bind.

The very characteristics of these pupils are God-given opportunities to win them to Christ. In the Sunday school, Sunday after Sunday, the teachers have before them in their classes those who are tenderhearted, trusting, gentle, free, frank, impulsive, unsettled, doubting, ambitious, aspiring. They believe the Bible to be the Word of God; they have faith in their teachers. It is the logical time for the alert, skilful, Spirit-filled teachers to lead them to Christ.

Again the mature people who are lost but are members of the Sunday school are far more susceptible to the convicting power of the Holy Spirit and can respond much more readily to the gospel call than can those who do not attend and who do not study the Bible.

4. *The Soul-winners of a Church Are Found in the Sunday School*

The members of the churches who are regular at the business of winning souls belong to the Sunday school. For co-operation in winning the lost people to Christ the pastor can rely upon the officers, teachers, and saved pupils in the Sunday school as upon no other members of his church. Pastors and evangelists everywhere testify that the people upon whom they must depend to help in winning people to Christ in their meetings are the officers and teachers in the Sunday schools and the members of the different classes.

This is true because in the Sunday school, more than anywhere else in the church, a Christian acquires the elements necessary for making a soul-winner. These elements are: the study of the Bible, the spirit of prayer and of work for others, constant thought and deep concern for others, and instruction in the art of soul-winning.

The intimacy existing between teachers and pupils and between fellow pupils still further emphasizes the Sunday school as a favorable soul-winning opportunity.

II. UTILIZING THE SOUL-WINNING OPPORTUNITY OFFERED IN THE SUNDAY SCHOOL

The foregoing statements simply set forth and emphasize a condition which exists in Sunday schools everywhere. The question of deepest importance is, How may this wonderful soul-winning opportunity offered in the Sunday school be utilized and be made practical?

1. *The Superintendent and Pastor Should Co-operate in a Soul-winning Program*

If the pastor is a soul-winner and finds himself with an unsympathetic, passionless superintendent on his hands, he will be greatly hindered in leading his teachers in the work of winning the lost. On the other hand, if the pastor does not co-operate with and encourage the superintendent, the Sunday school will fail as a soul-winning activity. The soul-winning desire must be strong in both the superintendent and pastor in order to have a Sunday school which is effective in soul winning.

In many churches the business of winning the lost to Christ is limited to an annual protracted meeting effort of one or two weeks' duration, led by an evangelist and singer. Good and blessed in results as scores upon scores of such meetings have been, this method alone is not an adequate soul-winning program for a church. It is not enough to meet the soul needs of the lost people in the community and to develop a soul-winning church.

The pastor and superintendent should have a program covering the entire fifty-two weeks in every year for winning the lost pupils in the Sunday school to Christ.

2. *Each Teacher Should Have a Prayer List of the Lost for Whom His Class Is Responsible*

Each teacher should have a prayer list both of the lost pupils in his class and of the lost who are prospects for his class. This list should be kept in the Bible and daily spread out before God as the teacher prays for each one by name. The pastor and superintendent should get the teachers to covenant together publicly to pray daily for their lost pupils. The habit of daily intercessory prayer will make over any Christian and any church, and cause streams of salvation to flow like rivers. Many Sunday school pupils can be reached only through prayer.

3. *The Salvation of the Lost Should Be a Matter of Prayer at Each Weekly Officers and Teachers' Meeting*

The plan suggested for an officers and teachers' meeting in this study contemplates bringing the officers and teachers of the Sunday school into the midweek prayer meeting, thus combining and mobilizing the working and praying forces of the church. There should be at least ten or fifteen minutes at the beginning of the prayer meeting for requests for prayer by teachers for their lost pupils and friends. This will furnish a definite objective for the prayer meeting. It will guarantee definiteness in praying, keep the soul-winning fires burning in the church, and greatly increase the value of the Sunday school as a soul-winning agency.

4. *Periods of Study and Special Effort Should Be Conducted*

Annually, or better semiannually, the officers, teachers, and saved pupils should be brought together for a week of study, prayer, and individual effort to win to Christ the pupils who are not Christians.

The class should be organized by the superintendent and taught, preferably, by the pastor. Persistent effort should be used to enrol all the officers and teachers and a large number of the saved pupils in the class. The Sunday school secretary should enrol the class and keep a close check on the attendance each evening.

The book to be studied should be placed in the hands of the members of the class several days in advance in order that they may read it through. There should be only one class, all taking the same book. The object of the study is not to get seals but to win souls.

The following books are suggested:

How to Win to Christ—Burroughs

The Way Made Plain—Brookes

Plan of Salvation—Crouch

Winning Others to Christ—Roland Q. Leavell

A Winning Witness—G. S. Dobbins

Soul-Winning Doctrines—Turner

The Place of the Sunday School in Evangelism—Barnette

One to Eight—Barnette

Such books as *Winning the Children* by Dobbins, and *Follow Thou Me* by Truett, will enrich those who use them for collateral reading.

In the event there are those who are not able to buy the books, the superintendent should lead the church in providing books for all such who promise faithfully to do the work.

Each member of the class should have a list of names of lost people for whom he promises to pray daily. Teachers would be interested most in their lost pupils, and members of the different classes in their lost fellow pupils. Not only should they pray for them, but they should definitely seek them out during the week and make an opportunity to speak to them about their souls.

This is pastor and people taking advantage of and utilizing the soul-winning opportunities offered in the Sunday school. This is pastor and people getting at the business of winning the lost and conserving the work of the teacher and preacher.

The work should run from Sunday to Sunday. The pastor may wish to preach the first Sunday on prayer and personal soul-winning. The class should meet each evening during the week, from Monday to Friday. The second Sunday should be a time of harvest.

The program submitted may be followed closely:

SCHEDULE OF WORK MONDAY THROUGH FRIDAY

6:15 Classwork—Led by the pastor
7:00 Supper, served free to all workers
7:30 Classwork as before supper
8:15 Reports and experiences from the members of the class
Requests for prayer
A season of prayer
8:30 Adjournment

At the close of the last period each evening the pastor should give an opportunity for reports and requests for prayer, closing with a season of special prayer led by many of the workers.

The reports should consist of the experiences of the different members of the class as they have gone to and fro praying with and speaking to their lost pupils and friends. As the week advances the reports will become more interesting and encouraging. Many happy incidents will be recited by the workers and answers to prayer will be reported.

Sunday morning at the Sunday school hour the teachers should teach with one purpose in mind and that to win the lost to Christ. Both the morning and the evening sermons of the pastor should have this objective. The messages should be direct and the invitations to accept Christ should be urgent. The teachers should see to it that their pupils attend the preaching service. They should sit with them, silently praying for them, and wisely influence them to act upon the invitation of the pastor. Does anyone doubt the results of an effort of this sort? Let him try it!

5. *Pupils Who Are Lost Should Attend the Sunday Morning Preaching Service*

It is absolutely essential that lost pupils attend the Sunday morning preaching service if the best results are to be had from the work of the teachers and pastors. To make an appeal to lost people when they are not there is like fishing for fish where there are no fish, or gunning for game that is gone. Therefore, if the pastor is to win lost people to Christ, he must have them before him when he preaches. Just here the Sunday school should furnish the pastor his Sunday morning audiences of lost people, and can be made to do so if the matter is gone about intelligently and vigorously.

Logically, the Sunday morning preaching service is the time and occasion for the pastor to win the lost to Christ. The surroundings and atmosphere are certainly most favorable for timid boys and girls and young men and women to yield to the pastor's invitation to accept Christ. The pupils come fresh from classes where they have been taught by godly teachers. They sit together in the preaching service in classes and departments with their teachers. The appeal of the pastor can easily be reinforced by a sympathetic glance, an earnest word, or a gentle pressure on the hand by a praying teacher or an anxious saved fellow pupil.

QUESTIONS FOR REVIEW

1. Give four reasons which emphasize the fact that the Sunday school is the church's greatest soul-winning opportunity.

2. Next to the pastor, who are the greatest soul-winners in the churches? Why is this true?

3. What is the first thing necessary in order to utilize the soul-winning opportunity offered in the Sunday school?

4. Suggest a practical method which all Sunday school teachers may use in winning their unconverted pupils to Christ.

5. Discuss the value of attendance upon the preaching service to pupils who are not Christians.

9

MEETINGS, EQUIPMENT, AND
RECORDS

Standard requirement:

1. *The school shall maintain a weekly officers and teachers' meeting or a monthly workers' conference.*

2. *The Sunday sessions of the school shall be at least one hour in length, preferably one hour and fifteen minutes.*

3. *Each age group below the Intermediates shall be separated from the remainder of the school, at least for the class sessions, by walls, movable partitions, screens, or curtains.*

4. *At least 50 per cent of the classes above the Juniors shall be separated from the remainder of the school for the class sessions by walls, movable partitions, screens, or curtains.*

5. *The school shall use the Six Point System.*

The requirement plainly states that the school shall maintain either a weekly officers and teachers' meeting or a monthly workers' conference. It is optional with the school as to which it shall have. However, it is almost impossible to maintain an effective Sunday school without a functioning weekly officers and teachers' meeting.

The need for a weekly officers and teachers' meeting has been intensified rather than diminished by the breaking up of the Sunday school into department groups, and the introduction of closely Graded Lessons. The complete success of the weekly officers and teachers' meeting in the past depended largely upon the method employed in conducting it. The same is true today.

It always has been difficult to maintain a real, live, interesting officers and teachers' meeting, and it is no more difficult now than it was before Graded Lessons came into use, if correct methods are employed.

In nowise should the officers and teachers' meeting take the place of the monthly workers' conference. Both are needed. The main difference between them is that the officers and teachers' meeting convenes weekly and has in it four elements—social, study, business, and devotional. The workers' conference meets monthly and has in it only three of these elements—namely: social, business, and devotional. However the monthly workers' council may be combined with the weekly meeting for one week out of each month.

I. The Purpose of the Weekly Officers and Teachers' Meeting

There are four well-defined purposes in the weekly officers and teachers' meeting. Let us consider them.

1. *To Promote Study of the Lesson for the Following Sunday*

Busy Sunday school teachers are prone to defer the study of the lesson until the last minute and, as a result, find themselves poorly prepared to go before their classes Sunday morning. Lack of interest, irregularity in attendance, and all-round poor work are inevitable in such cases.

A well-planned, well-conducted officers and teachers' meeting which meets not later than Wednesday each week will serve to correct this condition. The officers and teachers' meeting is an incentive to lesson study, and practically insures lesson preparation. It is absolutely essential if the highest standard of teaching is maintained throughout the Sunday school.

2. To Study How Best to Teach the Lesson

The best officers and teachers' meeting is a workshop, not a lecture. Not only should the lesson itself be reviewed, but it is also important that teachers should gain knowledge and skill in how to teach the lesson. Sunday school teachers need all the help they can get in this direction. The simple, practical plan presented herein admirably meets this need and sends the teachers away from the officers and teachers' meeting with concrete ideas for the presentation of the lesson. The inspiration to be gained from a good officers and teachers' meeting is of inestimable value and cannot be secured elsewhere.

3. To Consider Briefly the Problems of the School

A few minutes each week should be devoted to the consideration of the problems arising in the Sunday school which should not wait for the monthly workers' conference. The monthly workers' conference is a place to make and receive reports, determine policies, and adopt plans for carrying on the work of the school. The brief conference periods in the officers and teachers' meeting each week, both general and department, help in making these plans effective, keeping them before the officers and teachers, and offering opportunity for making announcements, asking questions, and making explanations when necessary.

4. To Pray

The need for praying Sunday school teachers is as great as the need for teachers who know what and how to teach. Every Sunday school teacher needs to pray. The help and the wisdom that come through prayer are to be had in no other way. Many Sunday school pupils can be reached only through prayer.

II. The Plan and the Program for the Weekly Officers and Teachers' Meeting

The plan and the program herein suggested may be adapted to any Sunday school in which the leaders are ready to put forth the needed effort. In some situations the lunch may be omitted. The order for the general and department conferences may be reversed, and the general conference held around the tables after the meal. In schools which are organized on the class basis, the general superintendent will be responsible for the work which is suggested here for the department period. However he should provide separate conferences during the teaching improvement period, as indicated on page 121.

Suggested Program for Wednesday Evening

6:00 p.m. Lunch, with social feature
    Announcements, projecting certain emphases
     for the department conferences
6:30 p.m. Department conferences
    1. Promotional Period, 15 minutes
    2. Teaching Improvement Period, 45 minutes
7:30 p.m. General conference, 15 minutes
    1. Reports from department conferences
    2. General promotional matters
    3. Special prayers
7:45 p.m. Regular prayer meeting—led by pastor

1. *Lunch*

The lunch may be furnished free by the church. However, many churches find that a nominal charge for the meal allows the parents to bring their children without embarassment. In such cases, the additional expense is provided for in the church budget. It is doubtful if a like sum invested elsewhere will result in equal returns in Christian fellowship, mutual encouragement, and unity.

2. Department Conferences

Promptly at 6:30 the meeting around the table should convene for the general conference if that comes first, or break up into department groups. These department conferences should be presided over by the department superintendent, according to a carefully planned program.

(1) *Promotional matters.*—Regular matters for attention each week would include the secretary's report and the needs it reveals; checking on progress toward accepted goals; written visitation reports and assignment of prospects; the assembly program for the next Sunday; and class activities. From time to time special emphasis would be given to such matters as Standards, working with parents, pre-session activities, Promotion Day, social activities, records, mission programs, visitation, training, and other activities based on the calendar adopted for the Sunday school.

(2) *Teaching improvement period.*—As a general rule the teaching improvement period will be conducted as a workshop where teachers plan together how to teach next Sunday's lesson. The department superintendent will lead them to evaluate last Sunday's teaching; look at the new lesson; consider pupil needs to be met; determine the teaching purpose; plan the steps in the teaching procedure; decide how to stimulate study of the lesson to follow.

The superintendent will find help for conducting this period in the pamphlet *How a Superintendent Develops Teachers,* by Corzine. (Available free from the State

Sunday school department or from the Sunday School Department, Baptist Sunday School Board, Nashville, Tennessee.)

In a department using Graded literature, where there is a different lesson for each year in the age group, one lesson may be selected for consideration. Sometimes there may be a demonstration lesson taught by one of the teachers, showing how he would teach this lesson to his class.

After the demonstration lesson, which should not require more than twenty minutes, there would be time to evaluate the teaching and to apply the principles which have been brought out to the other lessons to be taught in the department.

If there is a separate department for each year through the sixteenth there will be only one lesson to consider in each of these departments each week. This makes an ideal situation.

Superintendents of departments using the closely Graded Lesson Series will find help in their superintendents' manuals and in the teaching procedure outlined in the teachers' books for their respective age groups.

The Uniform Lessons are designed for use in all Adult and Young People's Departments; in Intermediate, Junior, and Primary departments which cannot offer separate classes for each year; and in all class Sunday schools. Most Sunday schools today need at least one department for each age group, even though there may be only two classes. In such cases the teaching improvement periods will be conducted by the department superintendents. The discussion will be based on the teaching procedure outlined in the periodicals for the teachers.

In the class Sunday school it may be necessary for teachers of Adults, Young People and Intermediates to meet together for the teaching improvement period. The leader of such a group may follow the procedure suggested in *The Sunday School Builder*, as he leads the workers in the use of their respective age group periodicals.

Teachers of Juniors and teachers of Primaries in a class Sunday school may meet together to compare the procedures outlined in their respective teacher's quarterlies, and to make their plans for Sunday. However, separate meetings are preferable.

Every Sunday school today needs separate departments for its Beginner and Nursery age groups. Superintendents for these age groups will use the teaching improvement periods to help their workers adapt and use the procedures outlined in their respective teachers' periodicals.

Separate conferences for the Cradle Roll department workers and for the Extension department workers should also be provided.

4. *General Conference*

In many churches the general conference is held immediately after the meal, while the workers are still at the tables. It is the time when the general superintendent promotes the Sunday school activities which are outlined in the Standard of Excellence, the church program, and the denominational calendar of activities. It is his opportunity to direct and harmonize the work of all the departments and classes, and to promote the whole program which the church has elected him to carry out.

III. BENEFITS OF THE WEEKLY OFFICERS AND TEACHERS' MEETING

We mention seven distinct benefits derived from the weekly officers and teachers' meeting. These benefits are really tremendous needs in every Sunday school and they can be more adequately met through a good weekly officers and teachers' meeting than in any other way.

1. *It Provides for a Good Time Socially*

It affords the Sunday school workers an opportunity to get together, and know each other better. In large Sunday schools the officers and teachers may not be acquainted with each other even in the same department, as there is no time for social intercourse Sunday morning. The officers and teachers' meeting offers an opportunity for fellowship among the workers. The lunch feature is especially designed with this end in view.

2. *It Affords Opportunity to Use the Six Point Record System*

Records are collected on Sunday morning; they are actually used when a group of workers study them to discover weak points in the Sunday school program. Records, rightly analyzed and interpreted, will help the superintendents and their co-workers to diagnose the needs of the whole school, the respective departments, the classes, and the individual pupils. The pupil's record will reveal personal needs and suggest objectives for visitation by the teacher or, in the case of Young People or Adults, the class officers.

The records of a class or a department reveal points on which there should be concerted emphasis. They may point to the need of increased visitation to enrol more members, to bring back absentees, to encourage individuals to be prompt, to enlist members in Bible study, to secure support of the church budget, or to encourage members to stay for preaching. Records may indicate that the assembly programs need to be made more worthwhile in order to challenge people to come on time. Records may indicate that the type of teaching needs to be changed in order to stimulate pupils to study their lessons and to bring and use their Bibles. Records may indicate the need for assembly programs on stewardship, the value of public worship, or the blessings of Bible study. The weekly officers and teachers' meeting and the monthly workers' council offer the opportunity to diagnose the needs revealed by the records and to plan remedial measures.

3. *It Affords Opportunity to Discuss Plans to Meet the Needs of the School*

In the conferences questions will be raised and conditions will be disclosed that will be of greatest importance to the pastor, general superintendent, and department superintendents in their planning for the school. The individual thinking of the officers and teachers will find expression. Their opinions will be valuable, helping the superintendent and pastor to discover and utilize the ability of the officers and teachers, individually and collectively, in the administration of the affairs of the Sunday school.

4. *It Helps to Co-ordinate the Work of All the Departments*

It assists each department in realizing its relation to each and all of the departments. It fosters and encourages school spirit and at the same time it cultivates department spirit. This is the inevitable result as the entire Sunday school is enlisted in activities which are part of the calendar of the church and the denomination. The officers and teachers' meeting is the place to combine the work of the whole school in harmonious action and to promote a unified program of work.

5. *It Insures Better Teaching*

A good officers and teachers' meeting is an absolute guarantee of better teaching in the Sunday school. The improvement that is made in the teaching in the Sunday school by a good officers and teachers' meeting would amply justify the expenditure of the time, money, and hard work necessary to maintain it. A good officers and teachers' meeting will transform poor teachers into good teachers and make good teachers better teachers.

6. *It Is the Pastor's Best Opportunity to Enlist and Utilize the Soul-winning Forces of the Church*

The soul-winners in every church, almost without exception, are to be found among the officers and teachers of the Sunday school and the members of the Adult and Young People's classes. The officers and teachers' meetings furnish the pastor an opportunity once each week to lay this holy task on their hearts and to pray and plan with them in a definite way to win to Christ the lost pupils in their classes. The Sunday school has in its membership both the soul-winners and the souls to be won.

7. *It Helps to Correct the Absent Teacher Problem*

The vast majority of Sunday school teachers who absent themselves from the Sunday school on Sunday morning do not do so because of necessity; they do so from choice. They do not deliberately plan to stay away; they want to attend; they fully expect to attend; but they delay their lesson preparation until the last minute and Sunday morning when the "last minute" arrives, it finds them unprepared. Then, on any sort of trivial or even imaginary pretext, they stay away from Sunday school. In nine cases out of ten, if the teachers who are absent from their places Sunday morning were prepared to teach, they would attend the Sunday school. A good weekly officers and teachers' meeting will correct the absent teacher problem in a great measure and reduce the need for supply teachers to a minimum.

8. *It Furnishes an Opportunity for Developing the Habit of Intercessory Prayer*

Every Sunday school teacher should have a list of the pupils in his class who are not saved. These should constitute his daily "prayer list" or at least a part of it. At the close of the lesson and leading into the regular prayer service, the superintendent or the pastor should give an opportunity for all who desire to make requests for prayer for their lost pupils and friends. Following a brief period of silent prayer together, short prayers should be led by teacher after teacher, remembering at the throne of mercy and grace those for whom requests have been made. Results are certain when there is agreement in prayer. Not only will lost people be saved but those who pray will also receive comfort, strength, and blessings untold (Job 42:10).

IV. Monthly Workers' Conference

A good monthly workers' conference possesses three fundamental characteristics: fellowship, business, and devotion. It is truly a great Sunday school builder, however, it is not equal to, nor is it a substitute for, a weekly officers and teachers' meeting.

Practically all that has been said about the weekly officers and teachers' meeting, except that which refers to lesson preparation, may be said concerning the monthly workers' conference. Therefore, it is not necessary to go into lengthy discussion of the monthly workers' conference, except to emphasize its value and make some practical suggestions concerning its conduct and support.

V. Values of the Monthly Workers' Conference

It arouses interest and enthusiasm among the officers and teachers and is responsible for their regular and prompt attendance upon all of the activities of the Sunday school.

It encourages and grows a department spirit which is essential to the highest efficiency.

It develops a spirit of sympathetic co-operation among the departments. This is inevitable as each department becomes familiar with the plans and aims of the other departments.

It affords the pastor and superintendent opportunity to acquaint the officers and teachers with all their plans for the Sunday school's enlargement and betterment.

It furnishes a place for the solution of all the problems confronting the school.

It is the place for receiving reports for the past month and planning for the work of the ensuing month.

VI. PROGRAM FOR A MONTHLY WORKERS' CONFERENCE

6:15 Lunch—Served free to the workers

Provide some good music and a little fun.

7:00 General Conference

1. Roll call by departments. Recognize department having largest proportion of workers present.

2. Special recognition and vote of thanks to those serving the lunch.

3. Department reports, presented by the superintendent of each department. In undepartmentized schools at this period reports would be made by each teacher. Reports should be completed on the chalkboard or mimeographed and distributed.

4. General report, presented by the general secretary.

    5. Remarks by pastor and superintendent, followed by a general discussion.

    6. Special matters of business. Plans for the next month. Items in the calendar of activities.

8:00 Department Conferences

Department superintendents in charge. They should plan for carrying out the suggestions made in the general conference and make special department plans for next month.

8:30 Adjourn

VII. THE SIX POINT RECORD SYSTEM

The effective use of the Six Point Record System will facilitate all that the Sunday school is trying to do for its members. It is a pupil-centered program, designed to reveal to teachers and officers the individual needs of the members, and to guide them in ministering to those needs. A full discussion of the spiritual objective of the system, and instructions for its effective use will be found in the book *The Six Point Record System and Its Use* by Noland.

QUESTIONS FOR REVIEW

1. State the fourfold purpose of the weekly officers and teachers' meeting.

2. How will attendance upon the weekly officers and teachers' meeting affect the work of the teachers?

3. What is the value of the department conferences?

4. Discuss the lesson period of the weekly officers and teachers' meeting where Graded Lessons are used.

5. Mention the benefits to be derived from a good officers and teachers' meeting.

10

TRAINING

Standard requirement:

1. *The school shall conduct at least one training school each year completing at least one book in the Sunday School Training Course.*

2. *At least 50 per cent of the officers and teachers, including the pastor or superintendent, shall hold an award for either* BUILDING A STANDARD SUNDAY SCHOOL *or* A CHURCH USING ITS SUNDAY SCHOOL.

3. *At least 50 per cent of the officers and teachers, including the pastor or superintendent, shall hold an award for at least one other book in the Sunday School Training Course.*

The Sunday School Training Course as promoted by the Sunday School Board includes all the training books offered for Sunday school workers, and the Standard requirement is based on the need for Sunday school workers to study these books. In checking up to meet this requirement of the Standard of Excellence, any credit on BUILDING A STANDARD SUNDAY SCHOOL or *A Church Using Its Sunday School* will be recognized. In addition to this, the requirement is that 50 per cent of the working force shall have credit for at least one other book in the Sunday School Training Course.

It is to be noted that the department books on teaching are now recognized in the Sunday School Worker's Diploma section.

Note that a training class for workers must be conducted during the year. This is a big thing in the requirement. This class must be conducted as part of the work of the individual church. A few of the officers and teachers participating in a city-wide or association-wide training school held in another church will not meet the requirement. The "officers and teachers" of the Sunday school is intended to mean the general officers and department officers and regular teachers. Class officers and substitute teachers are not included. Certainly all Sunday school leaders will attempt to go far beyond the simple requirements of the Standard on this point, realizing that the thorough training of an adequate force of workers is one of the big jobs in building a great Sunday school.

I. Securing Trained Workers—the Greatest Problem in Every Sunday School

Here we come face to face with the real problem in building a great Sunday school—the necessity of training officers and teachers. It is imperative that a Sunday school have a trained and intelligent corps of workers if it is to realize fully its responsibility of reaching the scores of unenlisted people in every community.

1. *Some Imaginary Problems*

It is not a problem of location. That is to say the building of a Standard Sunday school is not dependent upon the place in which the school is located. To be sure it requires greater effort to build a good Sunday school in some churches and localities than in others, but a study of the situation reveals the fact that all types of churches, without regard to their location, have good Sunday schools and likewise all types of churches, without regard to their location, have poor Sunday schools.

For example: Consider two country churches of about the same size, both in good communities, the same distance from the railroad. One will have a well-graded, well-organized, large, enthusiastic Sunday school; while the other church, located in as good community, with as large membership, with equal opportunities in every way, will have a small, poorly organized inefficient Sunday school. Why do not both of these churches maintain good Sunday schools?

One other comparison: There are two large city churches, similarly located; one has a well-organized, enthusiastic, efficient Sunday school with a regular attendance of fifteen hundred to two thousand members; the other has and has had for twenty years or more, a cold, unattractive, inefficient Sunday school of about four hundred members. Why do not both of these churches have finely organized, well-equipped, soul-winning Sunday schools?

It is clearly seen from these examples that building a great Sunday school is not dependent upon the school's location. That is not the real problem at all; we shall have to go further and look deeper into the question to get a satisfactory answer.

It is not a problem of pupils coming to Sunday school. There are a sufficient number of prospective pupils within easy reach of the Sunday schools to fill to overflowing practically all the church buildings everywhere. In fact, the present church buildings are not half large enough to take care of the people who should attend the Sunday school. People do not voluntarily attend Sunday school in large numbers. They never did. They never will. They do not come; they must be brought.

On every hand ignorance of the Bible is appalling. This is true both among grown people and children. It is not because there is a scarcity of Bibles. Bibles are plentiful, they are cheap and are found in practically every home. Neither are people ignorant of the Bible because they are not able to understand it, at least much of it. Each one for himself may learn to know a great deal that is in the Bible. People can learn the Bible, but they do not voluntarily study it. They never did and most probably never will. They will not study; they must be taught.

In all communities there are scores of lost people. They are within earshot of the gospel message week after week. Many of them live under the very shadow of the churches. They need Christ. They can be saved. Many of them want to be saved, but they do not seek the Saviour. They never did and the great majority of them never will if left to themselves. They do not seek; they must be sought.

2. *The Real Problem*

The preceeding discussion brings us to the real need, which is an organization of sufficient size made up of intelligent, skilful, Spirit-filled men and women who will bring the pupils into the Sunday school, teach them the Word of God, and win them to Christ. Thus the real problem of building a great Sunday school anywhere, under all conditions and circumstances is one of developing trained officers and teachers.

(1) *Need for trained officers.*—The officers occupy the places of leadership and chief responsibility. They set the standard of progress along all lines. The size of the school is governed by them. They largely determine the quality of the teaching done. They set the gauge for the soul-winning spirit and fervor of the Sunday school. The quality of work done by the teachers will not, cannot, rise higher than the ability displayed by the officers in the administration of the affairs of the Sun-

day school. It is impossible to build an efficient Sunday school with an ignorant, indifferent, untrained, lazy, cold set of officers. No corps of teachers can overcome a handicap like that.

It is not the purpose of this discussion to go into the duties of the Sunday school officers in detail. Suffice it to say that it requires intelligent, consecrated, energetic officers to build a great Sunday school. The pastor, superintendent, associate superintendent, secretary, and department officers—all of them—must know their duties. Each one must know what he is to do and how to do it. The Sunday School Training Course has been most carefully planned with this great fact in mind, and no officer need be ignorant about his work.

(2) *Need for trained teachers.*—The successful Sunday school teacher must know many things. He must know the Bible; he must know the pupil; he must know how to teach; he must know the art of class building; he must have a working knowledge of the science of general Sunday school administration; he must know how to win his lost pupils to Christ; he must know how to build Christian character; he must know the doctrines of his church; he must know how to lead his pupils out into service—and much more. Nothing less than a knowledge of all these things will meet the insistent demands made upon those who teach in the present-day Sunday school.

The pertinent question arises, Can busy men and women whose time is consumed with the legitimate pursuits of life meet these demands? The answer is, Multitudes of them are doing it gloriously. Another question comes with force, How are they able to do it? They are availing themselves of the help afforded by the books in the Sunday School Training Course which have been planned to meet their specific needs.

II. An Adequate Training Program—the Only Answer

Officers and teachers do not just naturally know their work and how to do it. And those who need to be enlisted as officers and teachers do not even know what it is all about and what they are being asked to do; so naturally they cannot appreciate the joys and privileges and benefits involved in the opportunity. If ever a Sunday school is to have an organization of officers and teachers that is large enough, and at the same time skilled in and consecrated to the work in hand, it will be largely the result of a comprehensive program of training carried on constantly. Three suggestions are made concerning any adequate program for training Sunday school workers.

1. *Training for the Present Organization and for a Prospective Force*

To maintain a growing organization of trained workers presents a twofold task and involves an enlarged conception of a training program for Sunday school workers. Of course, there must be the constant and intensive training of every regular officer and teacher in the Sunday school organization. No worker should either expect or be allowed to remain in the organization who refuses or neglects to take advantage of training for the purpose of improving the quality of his work. At the same time the leadership of the school is bound to offer constant opportunities and incentives for all officers and teachers to participate in training work.

In addition to the training of the present organization, there must be the constant effort to make the workers' training program of the school include a large number of prospective officers and teachers. The tremendous truth is that absolutely every member of the church needs training for service and every unenlisted member is a challenge to the Sunday school leadership. The church membership roll should be constantly and carefully studied and the names of those who possibly could make good workers, and who should be enlisted and trained, should be marked for special attention. Then in the organization and conduct of the training processes there should be provision of classes for these and the necessary enlistment effort put forth to get them into the training work. The enlistment of large numbers of new people and their careful training present the only possible method of providing at all times for an adequate force of workers.

2. Sufficient Time and Leadership

Here again is a twofold angle. Asked about the training opportunities provided for the workers in his Sunday school, a general superintendent said, "Why, we cooperate with the city-wide annual training school. Other than that we have no training work in our Sunday school!" As well try to train a young preacher by sending him to a convention once a year. As well expect a good crop from the field that gets rain only once a year. As well expect to make brick without straw, or to get success without effort, as to expect such a program of training to produce workers who know what and how to do the work of a Sunday school. Why, even if a teacher remained in service and never missed a single annual training school, it would take over twenty years for him to come anywhere near doing sufficient training to become an efficient teacher or officer.

Constant opportunities should be provided, with special weeks of training at least during each quarter, and other opportunities sandwiched in at every possible time. Time must be provided and insistent and continuous effort made to get the workers and prospective workers to be and remain engaged in the task of training for this all-important work.

The conduct of such a training program and the provision of time and courses will only come from the work of a consecrated and concentrated leadership. Every superintendent whose vision and desire is for the betterment of his school and the increase of its spiritual ministry will devote himself untiringly to this work of training, and will call to his aid all available forces of leadership. An associate general superintendent will be enlisted to lead this work specifically. The pastor will be called upon for his support and teaching ability. Special workers from the state Sunday school forces will be called in to teach special classes occasionally. And above all, teachers with ability to become teachers of teachers will be discovered within the membership of the church and will be committed and developed for this mighty task.

If ever this task of training present and prospective forces is to be accomplished, there absolutely must be the provision of sufficient time and leadership. Whatever investment is made here will pay dividends beyond computation in the enlarged outreach and improved spiritual ministry of a Sunday school.

3. *The Right Training Course Textbooks*

Almost anything and everything has been written in books concerning the administrative and teaching angles of Sunday school work. In training a group of workers, it is well to be able to guide them to the best sources of study in the realm in which they are at work. Here, as in the selection of Sunday school lesson literature, Baptists will do well to consider the textbooks for training Sunday school workers that have been prepared by Baptists, and which are devoted to the protection and promotion of Baptist doctrine and practice. Let us consider the training course offered and how it meets the needs of our work and our workers.

III. The Course Offered Meets the Needs of Sunday School Workers

1. *The Sunday School Training Course*

Combining the best wisdom of all our Sunday school leaders, the Sunday School Training Course offers a complete study in all phases of Sunday school work.

It is arranged in six sections, carrying a number of books under each. Thus a comprehensive and adequate course is offered, the mastery of which will be a challenge to all Sunday school leaders and workers throughout our territory and beyond.

For a leaflet listing all the books, write to the Sunday School Department, Baptist Sunday School Board, Nashville, Tennessee.

The names and the authors of the books in the Sunday School Training Course and a description of each book can also be found in *The Master Key* catalogue.

2. *The Needs*

The needs of Sunday school workers are common to all. The following discussion indicates some of them and indicates that the solution may be found through a careful study of the books in the course just described.

(1) *Pastors and superintendents who know the science of Sunday school building.*—Would pastors and superintendents know the science of Sunday school building? They can learn it by taking this Training Course. Very definitely some of these books tell how to build a Sunday school and all the steps incident thereto, such as:

How to take a religious census

How to organize the Sunday school

How to grade the Sunday school

How to maintain a weekly officers and teachers' meeting

How to conduct a monthly workers' conference

How to enlist and train teachers

How to have a good program every Sunday morning

How to keep the pupils for the preaching service

How to keep records and make reports

How to win the lost to Christ

All these and other vital topics dealing with Sunday school administration are dealt with in a practical way in this course.

(2) *Department superintendents who know how to put their departments on an efficient basis.*—Would department superintendents know how to put their departments on an efficient basis? Would they understand how to reach out and bring into the departments all those who should attend? Do they really care to learn how to conduct the department in such a way that every teacher can render the best possible service and every pupil receive the greatest possible good? They can most assuredly know all these things by mastering this course.

This course gives specific direction concerning the conduct of each department, from the Cradle Roll to the Extension department. It tells how to organize and equip each department, and how to deal intelligently with the pupils on the basis of their peculiar needs. Each department superintendent may become an expert in his particular field of labor and direct the activities of his department with the confidence and enthusiasm born of knowledge and skill.

(3) *Teachers who are skilled workmen.*—Would teachers know their Bibles? Would they know their pupils, how to teach them, how to win them to Christ, how to

enlist them in service and develop them in Christian character? By all means, teachers should study this course. By mastering even a few well-chosen books from this course a poor teacher can become a good teacher, and a good teacher can become a better teacher. "Study to shew thyself approved unto God, a workman that needeth not to be ashamed, rightly dividing the word of truth" (2 Tim. 2:15).

(4) *Teachers and class officers who know the science of class building.*—If teachers and class officers would know the science of class building, let them study the books in the Sunday School Training Course. By studying these books the teacher can know his place in building the class, how to advise, how to plan and co-operate with the officers in their plans for the class. Each officer can learn what his duties are and how to discharge them. Every member, by taking this course, can become intelligent and useful and fit himself for a wider field of service.

(5) *A trained army of officers and teachers.*—Would the pastor have in his Sunday school a group of men and women who know the Bible and how to use it? Let him consider carefully the possibilities of this course which has been planned to help him realize this very desire. What the theological seminaries, missionary training schools, and Bible institutes are doing for young preachers, missionaries, and vocational workers, the Sunday School Training Course can do, and, if thoroughly mastered, will do for Sunday school officers and teachers in churches everywhere. No Sunday school officer or teacher need longer be a bungler, if he will avail himself of the help it affords.

IV. METHODS OF PROCEDURE IN TRAINING WORK

We have considered the fact that the securing of skilled workers is the greatest problem in every Sunday school and that an adequate program of training is the only process through which to get these workers. We have seen that the Sunday School Training Course contains the textbooks best suited for use in training our workers. Now we come to some suggestions for the actual carrying on of this program of training.

1. *A Training Policy Should Be Adopted*

Every church should have a definite program for training the Sunday school officers and teachers; and this program should be led by the pastor and the superintendent. It should be purposeful, well-planned, and vigorously executed.

It should be made plain that all those who hold places of leadership and responsibility in the Sunday schools are expected to study and prepare themselves for this work.

Every church should make available in its library, copies of the books in the Sunday School Training Course. These books should be accessible to everyone in the Sunday school and to all workers who desire to study them privately.

2. *Definite Plans Should Be Utilized*

We offer suggestions as to how each church may train its own Sunday school officers and teachers as a part of its regular work. The following methods are being used with great success:

(1) *Individual study.*—The work may be carried on through individual study. The only thing necessary is to order the book desired and follow the instructions found near the back of the book. Send the written work to the state Sunday school secretary, and he will request the proper award. Thousands have and are doing the work in this way with results that are tremendously gratifying to all.

(2) *Special classes.*—Special classes may be held in the afternoon. This time appeals especially to the workers in the Extension, Cradle Roll, Nursery, Beginner, and Primary departments. A suitable time is usually about three or four o'clock in the afternoon. Ten periods of classwork of forty-five minutes each are required for completing a book. According to this plan a class meeting for one hour and a half each day from Monday to Friday could easily complete one of the department books in a week. This plan appeals particularly to workers who find it convenient to attend afternoon classes.

Another method is to designate one evening each week and meet on that evening for ten weeks. This will require enlistment and follow-up work, but offers the advantage of time for study between class periods.

(3) *Special weeks of training.*—Progressive churches need an intensive training plan for their Sunday school officers and teachers. They find it necessary in these busy days to offer many special weeks of training every year in order to make it possible for every officer and teacher to secure the training he needs.

In this way men and women are induced to take the work in large numbers. They study, they master their subjects, they qualify for the awards, and the results of their work afterwards verify the wisdom of doing the work this way.

Workers and prospective workers should be enrolled well in advance of the training school. The books should be on hand and as the workers are enrolled they should get a book and familarize themselves with it before the work begins.

In churches with department Sunday schools it is good to have all the department books taught simultaneously. If a church has not within its membership sufficient teachers to put on all the department books, often one or more of the denominational Sunday school workers may be secured, and neighboring pastors and teachers are often available.

Every church, and every worker, should consider it a point of honor to comply fully with the requirements for credit (see p. 147).

3. *A Program of Training Should Be Worked Out*

One training effort a year, or spasmodic training efforts will not meet the needs. A long-range, continuous program of training is essential. Include in this program the individual study plan, special training classes (as many as possible at stated hours throughout the year), and great weeks of special training as needed to accomplish the tasks at hand.

Whatever your program of training, plan it. Write it into the church calendar of activities at the beginning of the year. Nothing can help pastors and superintendents develop unity, spirit, and vision among their people better than a great program of training.

QUESTIONS FOR REVIEW

1. What is the real problem in building a Sunday school?

2. To what extent is the efficiency of the Sunday school dependent upon the officers?

3. Discuss the necessity for having an adequate training program. What two things should such a program provide?

4. What is said about every church having a definite training policy?

5. Mention three methods of doing training work, and discuss in detail the week of special training.

11

STEWARDSHIP AND MISSIONS

Standard requirement:

1. *The school shall support the church program and promote the general missionary, educational, and benevolent causes fostered by the denomination.*

2. *The school shall present educationally each year at least four denominational causes, and shall provide opportunities for the members to contribute to each of these causes in accordance with the policy of the church.*

As the first requirement of the Standard seeks right relationship between the Sunday school and the church of which it is a part, so this tenth requirement seeks to relate the Sunday school, through the church to which it belongs, to our worldwide Baptist denominational program. The requirement is simple and clear: Four of the great causes of the denomination shall be presented each year to the school through special programs, either by departments or to the school as a whole. The school shall provide opportunities for the members to contribute to these causes in accordance with the policy of the church.

Where the entire Sunday school offering each Sunday goes into a completely unified church budget, and where a specified percentage of all monies received on this budget is actually and regularly given to denominational causes, this can be interpreted as meeting part one of the requirement, inasmuch as a part of all that is ever given in Sunday school goes to missions. However, the mere fact that a Sunday school is a part of a church which has a regular unified budget which includes missions does not meet this requirement, the idea being that every member of the Sunday school shall have an opportunity and an invitation to give to these great causes. Definite programs should be planned to inform members on at least four denominational causes each year.

I. THE SUNDAY SCHOOL'S DENOMINATIONAL RESPONSIBILITY

1. *The Sunday School and the Church*

The Sunday school, as the teaching agency of the church to which it belongs, is under direct obligation to teach essential truths concerning the plans and programs of the church, and to lend its support to the enterprises which the church fosters. True, the primary business of the Sunday school is to teach the Bible; but teaching the Bible means far more than just acquainting people with what the Bible says. The Bible is truly taught only when its teachings are carried over into conviction and conduct.

Jesus commissioned his disciples (1) to go, (2) to make disciples, (3) to baptize them, (4) to teach and train them so that they might go and make more disciples, and baptize them, and teach and train them, so that they might go,—and in this continuous and ever-enlarging circle carry on what he began until his purpose shall be realized.

2. *The Sunday School and the Denomination*

A "denomination" is a body of Christians holding common basic doctrines, aims and practices, and banded together to do co-operatively what they could not do separately. Southern Baptists believe that Christ has entrusted to them a witness which will not be borne unless they bear it; a service that will not be rendered unless they render it; a message that will not be propagated unless they preach and teach it. But no individual or church can do this alone. There must be intelligent, voluntary, enthusiastic co-operation on the part of the whole body of like-minded believers.

To work together thus in fulfilment of Christ's command is not optional with New Testament churches. They must work together in carrying out their Master's program or be found unfaithful to their trust. To be missionary or non-missionary is not a matter of choice with a true Sunday school; if it is true to the Bible, a missionary Book; to the church, a missionary organization; and to Christ, the Great Missionary, a Sunday school must be missionary in spirit and practice.

3. *The Meaning of Missions*

By missions we mean simply going with the gospel and its fruits to those who are without Christ. The actual work of soul-winning we call evangelism. Missions is the broader term, and takes into account not only those who can be reached by our immediate personal witness, but also those who are at a distance, to whom we cannot bear personal witness, but must send our representatives. These representatives, who dedicate themselves at the call of Christ to go anywhere they are needed, we designate "missionaries."

Every church should be a missionary church and every Christian a missionary. A Sunday school should not only teach the Bible doctrine of missions, but should be actively engaged in the business of missions. The program of Jesus distinctly declares that we are to be his witness "in Jerusalem [local or district missions], in all Judaea [state missions], and in Samaria [home missions], and unto the uttermost part of the earth [foreign missions]." This program of Christ has never been changed, and no Christian or body of Christians has ever been exempted from this commission.

4. *Education and Benevolence*

Jesus was the great Teacher. He trained a little group of disciples ("learners"), whom he sent out to be teachers. Christianity is an intelligent religion, and while its appeal is to the heart, it is always to the heart through the head. Those who go forth to be Christ's representatives, whether in places of lay leadership, or as pastors and missionaries, should have the best possible preparation. Luther Rice, one of our first two American Baptist foreign missionaries, established a school in the homeland, and often referred to Christian education as the "seed corn of the kingdom." The great majority of our preachers and missionaries, and many of our greatest Baptist laymen and women, are the products of our Baptist schools.

Surely a Sunday school must stand for Christian education. Its state Baptist schools, and the seminaries and training schools should be known and loved by every boy and girl, man and woman, on its rolls. A goodly percentage of its young people should be encouraged to attend these Baptist institutions of learning, and gifts of money should be sent regularly for their support. We shall do well to remember the sober words of Dr. George W. Truett when he said, "Wisdom shall have fled from us if we ever abandon our Baptist schools."

Jesus went about doing good. He had compassion on the multitudes, but his compassion was not exhausted by weeping and words. He fed the hungry multitudes, he healed the sick, he gave speech to the dumb and hearing to the deaf and sight to the blind. He comforted and cheered the distressed, and restored the demon possessed to their right minds. He took little children in his arms and blessed them, and spoke bitter woe unto any who ignored or neglected them or caused them to stumble. On the Cross he made provision for his mother in her dependence. He declared that his servants are worthy of their hire, and laid upon his followers the sacred obligation of caring for the material needs of those whom he called as his ministers.

Can a church call itself truly Christian if it refuses to share in these Christly ministries? We continue the healing ministry of Jesus by means of our hospitals. We enter into the fellowship of Jesus' care for little children through our Children's Homes. We follow the example of Jesus in his concern for his undershepherds through the Relief and Annuity Board. Much else we may and must do individually and directly in our own communities. These forms of benevolences we share together as a great Baptist body, doing thus collectively what would be impossible individually. A church—and the Sunday school of that church—cannot rightfully claim obedience to its Master if it refuses or neglects to have a worthy part in the support of these enterprises so dear to the heart of Christ.

II. THE BAPTIST WAY OF WORKING

The Baptist way of working may be expressed in two words: *voluntary co-operation*. The details may, and will, vary from time to time, but the principle remains the same—the gifts of the many, large and small, are put together and distributed to the various boards and institutions in proportion to their service and need. If this is done wisely and systematically, with the great body of Baptist people enlisted, it results in worthy support, multitudes of souls saved, great successes achieved for Christ, and a spirit of enthusiasm and holy boldness throughout the entire denomination.

The secret of success may be summed up in three words: *information, inspiration, enlistment*. The people, from the youngest to the oldest, must be informed concerning these great enterprises. They must be inspired to study, to pray, to realize what it all means. They must be enlisted in systematic, sacrificial support. This is where the Sunday school comes in, and no Sunday school can be accounted "Standard" that has failed at this practical point.

III. THE SUNDAY SCHOOL MISSIONARY PROGRAM IN OPERATION

1. *The Causes Fostered by the Denomination*

Nine great objects are here listed for which Baptists are co-operatively responsible: (1) home missions, (2) foreign missions, (3) hospitals, (4) state Baptist schools, (5) ministerial relief, (6) ministerial education, (7) state missions, (8) Children's Homes, (9) Baptist papers. Every Baptist ought to be intelligent and concerned about every one of these great interests. The Standard of Excellence requirement is that at least four of these general causes be presented educationally to the school each year and that the school shall provide opportunities for the members to contribute to each of these. The school may select those objects on which this special emphasis will be placed in accordance with its judgment of need and opportunity. However, all deserve attention and so a further suggestion is made.

2. *The Adoption of the Calendar of Denominational Activities*

One reason why many Baptists know so little about denominational affairs is that many churches have no adequate, systematic plan for bringing to their people essential information. It may happen that months and even years pass in an otherwise well-regulated Sunday school with practically no reference to home missions, foreign missions, our Baptist hospitals, our Baptist schools and colleges, the work of the Relief and Annuity Board, our theological seminaries, state missions, the Children's Homes, the state Baptist papers and other publications.

Annually the Executive Committee of the Southern Baptist Convention prepares a denominational calendar with suggested mission emphasis somewhat as follows:

Home and foreign missions in March, culminating in "Missionary Day" on the last Sunday.

Hospitals in May.

Christian education in April and September.

State missions in October, culminating in "State Mission Day" usually on the last Sunday.

Child-care ministry, Thanksgiving Sunday.

State Paper Day, any Sunday in November.

Every-member canvass on Sunday set by church.

For effectiveness, it is recommended and urged that a calendar similar to this be devised and adopted according to the judgment and leadership of the pastor and superintendent. The Standard requirement is that at least on four special occasions one or more of these causes be presented educationally, with an offering from the members.

3. *Prayer and Information Concerning These Causes*

The use of the denominational calendar keeps ever before the officers and teachers and members of the departments and classes the privilege and duty of definite prayer for certain great objects. On one Sunday the names of certain missionaries might be mentioned, and prayers offered on their behalf; on another Sunday prayer might be made especially for the hospitals and the sick and suffering whom they minister; on another Sunday there might be prayer for the Baptist schools of the state, the names of certain of the teachers and other workers in these institutions being mentioned; on another Sunday attention might be called to the theological seminaries and training schools, and prayer offered for their faculties and students; on another Sunday the work and beneficiaries of the Relief and Annuity Board might be remembered in prayer; the state and its need, and the work and workers of the State Mission Board should be frequently carried to the throne of grace. Surely at the Thanksgiving season the prayers of our hearts will rise to the Father on behalf of the children in our Baptist Children's Homes. On at least one Sunday the state paper and its editor, and other approved Baptist publications should be mentioned and made the object of earnest prayer. Christmas time should well be a time of prayer for more missionaries on all our great world fields to tell the story of the coming of the Saviour to those who have never heard it.

4. *Presenting the Causes Educationally*

The plan of educational presentation of these causes is simple and practical. Brief, attractive program material is sent regularly by the Home and Foreign Mission Boards and by the state mission boards to the Sunday school superintendents of each state. These programs may also be found in *The Sunday School Builder*, a monthly publication of the Sunday School Board. From time to time in accord with the calendar suggested, program material dealing with the other general causes will appear in *The Sunday School Builder*.

Pastor and superintendent may appoint competent individuals to take the available material and prepare opening and closing programs for the school as a whole, or as a "special feature" of each department in a department school. The teaching of the lesson will not be interfered with, but the usual time allotted for the assembly program will be devoted to an effective presentation, in vivid and instructive fashion, of a brief program on missions, or education, or benevolence. Such a program should utilize any missionary applications inherent in the regular Bible lessons of the day. Surely life and enthusiasm will be added to the assembly through this process, and these missionary programs will be a welcome feature to officers, teachers, and pupils alike.

The programs may be varied by an occasional brief address by a well-qualified speaker presenting one of the denominational causes, followed by a season of prayer for the object under consideration. Long experience has taught that the best plan is the rendering of a special program by selected individuals, utilizing the materials found in *The Sunday School Builder*.

With all this in mind, tracts may be ordered and distributed bearing on the special causes under consideration. Attractive posters may be prepared as projects by various classes, and posted conspicuously. Blackboard outlines and mottoes may speak their silent messages. Teachers may relate the lesson for the day to the special object, making it a point of contact for beginning the lesson, or an opportunity for practical application, or a source of helpful illustration. Officers and teachers who have the matter on their hearts, and who plan in advance, will find it delightfully easy to get fruitful information to the school regarding all our great denominational enterprises.

5. *The Offering an Essential Feature*

No learning is complete until it is put into practice. When the denominational causes are effectively presented, a desire to support them is awakened, or deepened. It is an important part of the educational process that every individual shall have an opportunity to respond by giving to the cause which has been presented.

If it is the custom of the school to take an offering other than the regular church offering, or if there will be members of the Sunday school who will not have the privilege of giving to the special cause through the church budget, then they should be given an opportunity to make a special offering in the Sunday school.

Several simple plans may be followed. The school may give its entire collection on this day as a special offering to the mission cause presented. Another good plan is to pass out special offering envelopes (which usually are furnished free by the state mission headquarters), in which an extra contribution will be placed.

It is the practice of many of our best churches to receive annual pledges to the church budget from all members of the Sunday school from Nursery age up. Each individual makes his weekly offering during the first service he attends on Sunday. Thus Sunday school pupils will make their church offering at the Sunday school hour. When this practice is followed, the members may be reminded, during the special mission program, that part of the love gifts in their envelopes each Sunday is used for the cause presented.

The fact that the church of which the Sunday school is a part gives to some or all of these causes through a unified budget does not fulfil the requirement except in cases where the whole Sunday school offering is a church offering and goes into a whole unified church treasury which actually gives a specified percentage of all monies received to missionary work. The purpose is to cultivate the grace of giving to missions on the part of every member of the Sunday school, and this can be accomplished only as the Sunday school itself accepts responsibility for definite giving.

IV. MAKING THE MOST OF THE DENOMINATIONAL DAYS

In connection with the development and use of the missionary calendar, it is expected that March and

October will become the two outstanding missionary months in a Sunday school's program and that the other special days will be observed as widely as possible.

The observance of each one of these great days should be Convention-wide. The aim is to reach every one of our Baptist Sunday schools.

Every pastor and superintendent should thoroughly inform himself concerning these plans to educate and to train our Sunday school membership along denominational lines. These leaders should put themselves positively back of these special day programs, and lead their forces to plan intelligently and prepare thoroughly for each one of these great days.

Much of the success of these special days depends upon the care and thoroughness with which the programs are prepared. Material is furnished for the largest or the smallest school. Good judgment must be used in selecting and adapting the material to meet the needs and capabilities of pupils. The program may be rendered at the regular morning preaching service, in a joint Sunday school assembly, or in the departments.

The preparation for the program should begin at least one month in advance. A competent committee should be put in charge that will give out the parts and arrange for weekly rehearsals so that the program may be rendered in the most effective way. They should see that parts are well learned, and that those who have them speak distinctly enough to be heard anywhere in the auditorium.

The offering is an essential feature of these programs, and under no circumstances should it be allowed to go by default. A special place should be made on the program for the offering or for explanation of how the cause is included in the church budget. It is sound educational practice to give pupils an immediate opportunity to express the attitudes and resolves aroused.

QUESTIONS FOR REVIEW

1. Discuss the importance of educating and training our Sunday schools along denominational lines and tell why Sunday school pupils should be asked to give to missions and benevolences.

2. Give two words which describe the Baptist way of working.

3. Tell how a Sunday school may present the various denominational causes educationally.

4. Why is the offering an essential feature of the denominational missionary occasions?

5. Suggest ways of making the most of these denominational days.

DIRECTIONS FOR THE TEACHING AND STUDY OF THIS BOOK FOR CREDIT

I. DIRECTIONS FOR THE TEACHER

1. Ten class periods of forty-five minutes each, or the equivalent, are required for the completion of a book for credit.

2. The teacher should request an award on the book taught.

3. The teacher shall give a written examination covering the subject matter in the textbook. The examination may take the form of assigned work to be done between the class sessions, in the class sessions, or as a final examination.

Exception: All who attend all of the class sessions: who read the book through by the close of the course; and who, in the judgment of the teacher, do the classwork satisfactorily may be exempted from taking the examination.

4. Application for Sunday school awards should be sent to the state Sunday school department on proper application forms. These forms should be made in triplicate. Keep the last copy for the church file, and send the other two copies.

II. DIRECTIONS FOR THE STUDENT*

(*The student must be fifteen years of age or older to receive Sunday school credit.)

1. In Classwork

(1) The student must attend at least six of the ten forty-five minute class periods to be entitled to take the class examination.

(2) The student must certify that the textbook has been read. (In rare cases where students may find it impracticable to read the book before the completion of the classwork, the teacher may accept a promise to read the book carefully within the next two weeks. This applies only to students who do the written work.)

(3) The student must take a written examination, making a minimum grade of 70 per cent, or qualify according to *Exception* noted above.

2. In Individual Study by Correspondence

Those who for any reason wish to study the book without the guidance of a teacher will use one of the following methods:

(1) Write answers to the questions printed in the book, or

(2) Write a development of the chapter outlines.

In either case the student must read the book through.

Students may find profit in studying the text together, but where awards are requested, individual papers are required.

All written work done by such students on books for Sunday school credit should be sent to the state Sunday school secretary.

III. THIS BOOK GIVES CREDIT IN SECTION II OF THE SUNDAY SCHOOL TRAINING COURSE